W9-ASK-290

THE ROLLER COASTER OF UNEMPLOYMENT

Sarah Hupp

with Michael Hupp

THE ROLLER COASTER OF UNEMPLOYMENT

Trusting God for the Ride

DISCOVERY HOUSE
PUBLISHERS®

Feeding the Soul with the Word of God

© 2010 by Sarah M. Hupp
All rights reserved.

Discovery House Publishers is affiliated with RBC Ministries,
Grand Rapids, Michigan.

Discovery House books are distributed to the trade exclusively by
Barbour Publishing, Inc., Uhrichsville, Ohio.

Requests for permission to quote from this book should be directed to: Permissions
Department, Discovery House Publishers, P.O. Box 3566, Grand Rapids, MI 49501.

Scripture quotations marked ESV are taken from *The Holy Bible, English Standard
Version*. Copyright © 2000, 2001 by Crossway Bibles, a division of Good News
Publishers. Used by permission. All rights reserved. Scripture quotations marked
GNT are taken from the Good News Translation® (Today's English Version, Second
Edition). Copyright © 1992 American Bible Society. All rights reserved. Scripture
quotations marked GOD'S WORD are taken from GOD'S WORD®. Copyright 1995 God's
Word to the Nations. Used by permission of Baker Publishing Group. Scripture quo-
tations marked HCSB are taken from the Holman Christian Standard Bible ® Copy-
right © 2003, 2002, 2000, 1999 by Holman Bible Publishers. Used by permission.
All rights reserved. Scripture quotations marked MSG are taken from *The Message*.
Copyright © 1993, 1994, 1995, 1996, 2000, 2001, 2002. Used by permission of Nav-
Press Publishing Group. Scripture versions marked NASB are taken from the NEW
AMERICAN STANDARD BIBLE®, Copyright © 1960, 1962, 1963, 1968, 1971, 1972,
1973, 1975, 1977, 1995 by The Lockman Foundation. Used by permission. Scripture
quotations marked NCV are taken from the New Century Version. Copyright ©
2005 by Thomas Nelson, Inc. Used by permission. All rights reserved. Scripture
quotations marked NIV are taken from the HOLY BIBLE, NEW INTERNATIONAL
VERSION®. Copyright © 1973, 1978, 1984 Biblica. Used by permission of Zonder-
van. All rights reserved. Scripture quotations marked NKJV are taken from the New
King James Version. Copyright © 1982 by Thomas Nelson, Inc. Used by permission. All rights reserved. Scripture quotations marked NLT are taken from the Holy
Bible, New Living Translation, copyright 1996, 2004. Used by permission of Tyndale
House Publishers, Inc., Wheaton, Illinois 60189. All rights reserved.

Interior design by Sherri L. Hoffman

Library of Congress Cataloging-in-Publication Data

Hupp, Sarah M.
The roller coaster of unemployment: trusting God for the ride / by Sarah
    M. Hupp, with Michael Hupp.
        p. cm.
ISBN 978-1-57293-376-7
1. Unemployed—Religious life. 2. Job hunting—Religious aspects—
    Christianity. I. Hupp, Michael. II. Title.
BV4596.U53H87 2010
248.8'8—dc22   2009053292

Printed in the United States of America

10 11 12 13 14/10 9 8 7 6 5 4 3 2 1

The Lord *is good, a refuge in times of trouble. He cares for those who trust in him.* NAHUM 1:7 NIV

This book is dedicated to Val Buick for the spark of her creativity and her confidence in my ink and paper. It has been a blessed ride.

CONTENTS

INTRODUCTION

They cried out to the Lord in their trouble, and he brought them out of their distress. PSALM 107:28 NIV

When my family and I arrived at the amusement park, I teased to go on the Dragon Coaster. I had seen the advertisements on television that showed the dragon-like shape of the twisted, twirly, mountainous roller coaster. Now I could hardly wait to get through the lines and board the ride so I could experience the fun for myself.

Unfortunately I was only seven years old, and I had never ridden a roller coaster before. Though my family had tried to warn me about how scary roller-coaster rides can be, I didn't have a clue about what all their talk meant. I just giggled excitedly during the wait time and teased to be allowed to sit with the big kids in the front of the car when we chose our seats.

As the ride began, the roller coaster car clanked and smoked (like a dragon) and chugged up the tallest hill I had ever been on. I could see the entire amusement park laid out below. I chattered even more, pointing out the wonderful sights to my seatmates.

But as the car reached the top of that first hill, my chattering came to an abrupt halt. I couldn't see any more track in front of me. I didn't know what to expect. When the coaster topped the hill and started to whoosh down the other side, you wouldn't believe the screams that escaped my lips. The twists and turns that had looked so innocent and simple to me while

I was waiting for the ride to begin now felt intimidating and scary. The ride along the twisty, green corkscrew track that had looked like so much fun now set my stomach churning, threatening to take my lunch away. Though the ride lasted fewer than two minutes, it ruined the rest of my day at the park, leaving me exhausted and too scared to try anything new.

When you lose your job, whether for rightsizing, business closures, a poor economy, or just because your boss had a bad day, the days spent between losing your old job and finding a new one can seem a lot like a bad roller-coaster ride. You're on that roller coaster even though you might not want to be, and now you have to ride that hill for all it's worth. You try to hold on tight as you navigate the twists and turns, excited at the possibility of a new job, an interview, or a lead. But then you're tumbled all around with disappointment when the phone stays silent for days on end, when no one returns your e-mails, when all the leads dry up. The dark fear of the unknown is like a roller-coaster tunnel with no bright sunshine of a job in sight. One day you're up; the next day you're down. The thought of it all leaves you exhausted and sick to your stomach. I should know. Unemployment has happened to my husband and me four times.

Well, if this is where you find yourself too, take heart. The Bible says when God's children call out to Him in their distress, He hears and comes to their aid. Sometimes He acts instantaneously, but sometimes His timetable takes a little longer. Yet He is always faithful to provide for His children. While you're waiting for His plan to unfold, my hope is the Bible verses, inspirational stories, helpful checklists, journal-style questions, and encouraging words in this book will help you ride *The Roller Coaster of Unemployment*.

God's blessings be yours.

—S. M. Hupp

1

CLIMBING THE HEIGHTS

Two fellows were waiting in front of me at the unemployment center. As the line slowly moved forward toward the career counselors' desks, I overheard one fellow say to the other, "I didn't expect this to happen, did you?" The second man only grunted his reply, so the first fellow continued, "I mean, I had a good job. A steady paycheck with a big company. Good benefits. Now look at me. I'm supposed to live on a paltry unemployment check. And, to get *that* I have to wait in these endless lines at this career center every week. I never expected all this!"

I could relate to that man. The unexpected changes in my own employment situation had left me feeling like I was on a roller-coaster ride. Yet as I thought about this man's words, I almost wanted to ask him, "Well then, what *were* you expecting?"

You see, too often when your paycheck is regular, your work is satisfying, and your coworkers are tolerable, you can assume your job will last forever. After all, your parents or grandparents might have worked for the same company for thirty or forty years without a layoff; why shouldn't you? Unfortunately, in today's society individuals will probably change jobs every three to four years over the course of their working lifetime. That means your employment ride will be more like an up-and-down roller-coaster ride than a slow and steady buggy trip through the park.

That also means you'll probably resemble a roller-coaster rider in some ways, too. Just as a roller-coaster rider spends time waiting in line for a thrill ride, you probably spent some time waiting for the last job you held, waiting for a reply to your application, waiting for an interview. But when you got the job, you unknowingly stepped from a waiting line right into a roller-coaster car. When you took home that first paycheck, whether you realized it or not, you automatically got strapped into a ride just like modern-day roller-coaster riders get strapped into their seats. The restraints on a coaster car that keep riders in their seats are just like the necessities of food and housing that kept you strapped into your job for its income and health benefits.

Yet you probably didn't think there would be a downside when you started your last job. You were probably more like those roller-coaster riders who were cheering and waving as they started climbing the heights of that first hill. Coaster riders are thrilled to be starting out. They're committed to the ride and are full of excitement and anticipation. They have no idea where the ride will take them, but it sure feels great to begin.

Why not let a little of the excitement of the beginning of a roller-coaster ride seep back into your heart, for regardless of whether you're unemployed or underemployed right now, God is still actively working on your behalf. Let the surety of that news keep you on track as this roller-coaster ride of unemployment begins. Once again climb the heights in anticipation of what God will do in and for you as you look at what He has to say about priorities, change, work, finances, and stress.

PRIORITIES

Your Top Priorities

Jehoshaphat also said to the king of Israel, "First seek the counsel of the LORD." 1 KINGS 22:5 NIV

Unemployment changes everything, doesn't it? Even your priorities are affected. When you had your last job you knew what your priorities were. You'd wake to a jangling alarm, get cleaned up, dressed, fed, watered, and out the door so you could get to your job on time. But now what should you do? You're frustrated, angry, bitter, and would love to mouth off to someone, but you can't do that. A neighbor said he spent eight hours every day looking for work. Should you spend all of your time that way? A friend's brother-in-law put his house up for sale to forestall a mortgage foreclosure. Should selling your house be your top priority? Should you stand on the street corner with a sign that says "Hire me!"? Should you take that job at McDonald's? Should you listen to every piece of advice everyone is giving you? Or should you crawl back into bed and pull the covers over your head?

Why not take a look at David instead? Before he was crowned king of Israel, he was on King Saul's most-wanted list. David and a small army of supporters moved to Ziklag, a town just outside Saul's reach. While David and his men were away from home helping Ziklag's leaders with an enemy skirmish, a band of marauders invaded Ziklag and burned the place. They carried off anything of value, too, including the women and children. When David and his men returned home to Ziklag, they found it destroyed and their families kidnapped.

What happens next, though, is significant. David's top priority wasn't retaliation or instant action. The Bible says David's first priority was to get his emotions out of the way. He and his men immediately "wept aloud until they had no strength left to weep" (1 Samuel 30:4 NIV). It was the same for Nehemiah when he learned about Jerusalem lying in ruins (Nehemiah 1:4). The Bible says he wept for days on end. And it was the same for Jesus when he learned that a good friend had died. The Bible says Jesus wept (John 11:35).

But after David wept, the Bible says he prayed and strengthened himself in God. After Nehemiah wept, he prayed. And after Jesus wept over Lazarus's death, the Bible says He prayed too. And when God came first in these men's lives, miracles happened. David was able to rescue the kidnapped families. Nehemiah was able to rebuild Jerusalem's walls. And Jesus brought Lazarus back to life. All because their priorities were right. They got rid of their emotional baggage and laid everything out in prayer to God before doing anything else.

How about you? Have you gotten the emotions attached to your job loss out of your heart? Folks respond differently to disappointments like unemployment, but to successfully survive this time in your life you need to let go of those emotions. Pummel the daylights out of a feather pillow. Holler your frustrations at the moon. Whatever it takes, weep until you can weep no more. And then, like David, Nehemiah, and Jesus, take time to pray. Tell God exactly where you're coming from. He knows it already, so don't try to fudge it or make it look any better than it is. Be honest. Ask Him what to do next. Make tears and prayer your top priorities and watch God do something wonderful in your life.

Getting Through Your Day

Thus says the Lord, *"Stand by the ways and see and ask for the ancient paths, where the good way is, and walk in it; and you will find rest for your souls."* Jeremiah 6:16 NASB

Above all, you must live as citizens of heaven, conducting yourselves in a manner worthy of the Good News about Christ. Then, whether I come and see you again or only hear about you, I will know that you are standing together with one spirit and one purpose, fighting together for the faith, which is the Good News. Philippians 1:27 NLT

Watch your step. Use your head. Make the most of every chance you get. These are desperate times! Don't live carelessly, unthinkingly. Make sure you understand what the Master wants. Ephesians 5:15–17 MSG

Set your mind on things above, not on things on the earth. For you died, and your life is hidden with Christ in God. Colossians 3:2–3 NKJV

Above all else, guard your heart, for it is the wellspring of life. Put away perversity from your mouth; keep corrupt talk far from your lips. Let your eyes look straight ahead, fix your gaze directly before you. Make level paths for your feet and take only ways that are firm. Do not swerve to the right or the left; keep your foot from evil. Proverbs 4:23–27 NIV

What does the Lord *require of you? To act justly and to love mercy and to walk humbly with your God.* Micah 6:8 NIV

Jesus answered, "'Love the Lord your God with all your heart, all your soul, and all your mind.' This is the first and most important command. And the second command is like the first: 'Love your neighbor as you love yourself.'" MATTHEW 22:37–39 NCV

Today I Will...

✓ Be thankful that God is aware of all my needs and has promised to take care of me.

✓ Be grateful for my former place of employment.

✓ Appreciate the friends and family who want to help, even though their suggestions may not always be as helpful as they think they are.

✓ Be pleased to remember that God is not annoyed or upset with my rantings and ravings. I can spill out my emotions to Him about my job loss and my future and He will still love me and listen.

✓ Be glad about the examples of David, Nehemiah, and Jesus, knowing that the same loving heavenly Father who worked on their behalf stands willing and able to bring about wonderful things for me too.

✓ Value the newness of greater trust in God because of this time of job loss. If things had kept on the way they were, I might not have sought God as deeply as I am seeking Him and His ways now.

CHANGE

Is God Mad at Me?

As Jesus passed by, He saw a man who was blind from birth.
And His disciples asked Him, saying, "Rabbi, who sinned, this man
or his parents, that he was born blind?"   JOHN 9:1–2 NKJV

My grandmother never smoked, drank, or cursed. She was faithful in church attendance, sang in the choir, and contributed heavily to charity efforts. She was a hard worker and lived within her means. Yet when the furnace quit one winter day, Grandmother was positive that God was mad at her. When she slipped on a wet floor a few weeks later and sprained her ankle, she was convinced that God was peeved about something yet again. And when my grandfather lost his job, that was the clincher. God really and truly had to be mad at her about something big, bad, or ugly.

Ever felt that way? When everything's going great God must be happy with you, but when things change and a job disappears then God must be mad at you for some reason, right? It's a normal enough feeling. After all, in the Bible, God's people were blessed when they did what He wanted. They didn't get hardships in return for right living. Therefore, if you lose your job, if the income stops coming in, if the changes that come your way are bad ones, it must be because God is mad at you, right? Not necessarily.

While the Bible does indicate that God will bring calamity on those who do not follow His ways, only you and God truly know whether you fall into that category. If you have habitually chosen your own way over God's way, if you have disregarded God's instructions and lived to gratify yourself, if you have set yourself up as the master of your own fate, God might be angry with you. The Bible says repentance is in order for those types of decisions.

But if, however, you are a child of God who consistently seeks to live by His ways, the hard, unexpected changes that come into your life are probably not signs that God is mad at you. The Bible says there's probably another reason for the changes that have taken place in your life.

When Jesus and His disciples came upon a blind man beside the road, the disciples asked Jesus who was being punished because the man was blind. Was God mad at the parents and punishing them, or was He mad at the blind man and punishing him? Jesus' answer surprised everyone. He said no one had sinned. God wasn't mad at anyone. As He prepared to heal the man Jesus proclaimed, "This happened so that the work of God might be displayed in his life" (John 9:3 NIV).

The world looked at the blind man and saw punishment and God's anger. But Jesus told His disciples to change their viewpoint, to look at things through God's eyes. The man's blindness was God's opportunity to bring glory to His name.

The same is true for you. God wants to shine brightly through your life. He wants His glory to be reflected in everything you do, in every situation you encounter. When life's hard changes come your way, these changes can be God's opportunities for greater growth and blessing in your life. You just need to change how you view change. Ask God to give you His view on your life changes. Let Him heal your viewpoint so that He can display His work in your life too.

Getting Through Your Day

Do not be conformed to this world, but be transformed by the renewing of your mind, so that you may prove what the will of

God is, that which is good and acceptable and perfect.

ROMANS 12:2 NASB

Every good gift and every perfect present comes from heaven; it comes down from God, the Creator of the heavenly lights, who does not change or cause darkness by turning.   JAMES 1:17 GNT

I am about to do something new. See, I have already begun! Do you not see it? I will make a pathway through the wilderness. I will create rivers in the dry wasteland.   ISAIAH 43:19 NLT

Then I saw a new heaven and a new earth, for the first heaven and the first earth had passed away, and there was no longer any sea. I saw the Holy City, the new Jerusalem, coming down out of heaven from God, prepared as a bride beautifully dressed for her husband. And I heard a loud voice from the throne saying, "Now the dwelling of God is with men, and he will live with them. They will be his people, and God himself will be with them and be their God. He will wipe every tear from their eyes. There will be no more death or mourning or crying or pain, for the old order of things has passed away." He who was seated on the throne said, "I am making everything new!" Then he said, "Write this down, for these words are trustworthy and true."

REVELATION 21:1–5 NIV

Today I Will Get This Off My Chest...

Use the space below to respond to as many or as few of the following questions as you like.

* Is God always with you through all the aspects and changes of life? Can He be trusted even when things change unexpectedly?

- How do you respond to change? What plan can you put into place to remind yourself to handle future changes with a better attitude?
- Have you done something you regret because of your recent job change? What can you do to make the situation better? Do you need to apologize to someone or make restitution?
- Can you think of one time in your life when change was a good thing? What was significant about this event? How can this apply to the changes you face now?

WORK AND CAREER

Trusting God for Your Work

*The LORD God put the man in the garden of Eden
to care for it and work it.* GENESIS 2:15 NCV

If you didn't have to work to pay the bills, feed the tater tots, and keep a roof over your head, you wouldn't work, would you? Well, would you? Amazingly, you just might. Often those who acquire large amounts of cash continue to work at their jobs. They've found life to be unfulfilling without a job more demanding than the steady clicking of a television remote control. A vacation from a job is one thing, but day after day of doing nothing will drive a sane person crazy.

There's a reason for this. When God created human beings, He created them with the innate need to do something, to be useful and productive. Because of that human need, the Bible says God set Adam up in the landscaping business, working in the garden of Eden. It was a great job, too. Adam would work all day and then walk with God in the evening. Great hours. Great benefits. And a great feeling to be useful.

People have felt the urge to work ever since because work is still a part of God's plan for His children. That's why when you find yourself without work, you often find yourself at loose ends. You want to be busy. You want to be useful and productive. But your job has just ended. So what are you to do?

Consider a Bible fellow named Bezalel. As a twenty-something, Bezalel had worked in Egypt making bricks for Pharaoh's building projects. When God delivered the Israelites and their herds from Egypt, Bezalel faced a job change. It wasn't something he had anticipated, yet the career move from slave to shepherd was probably welcome.

However, God wasn't finished with Bezalel. Unbeknownst to the young man, another job awaited him. The Bible says God had gifted Bezalel with "skill, ability and knowledge in all kinds of crafts" (Exodus 31:3 NIV). Those gifts didn't have a chance to blossom in Egypt's mud pits or in the sheep fields. But when God told Moses to build a worship center for God's people, Bezalel's gifts were in demand. The young man was given the job of making the ark, the place where God's presence would come and rest among His people. This new job brought added glory to God and greater satisfaction to Bezalel too. Because Bezalel had quietly trusted God, God had provided for him in an amazing way.

So what does that mean to you? God has created you, just like Adam, with an urge to work. He has given you a need to feel productive and useful. It's in your bones. God knows that. But right now you don't have day-to-day employment. God knows that, too, so He has given you the example of Bezalel. Bezalel's life experience is a reminder that jobs come and jobs go. Unemployment happens.

Yet re-employment also happens. You can use this time of unemployment to trust God, just like Bezalel did, and work. That's right—work. Work on your relationship with God, on your understanding of how He made you. Ask Him to show you your skills and abilities, to open your heart to new job possibilities that could bring Him greater glory. Then trust God to do for you what He did for Adam and Bezalel. Trust God to find you work.

Getting Through Your Day

Sow your seed in the morning, and at evening let not your hands be idle, for you do not know which will succeed, whether this or that, or whether both will do equally well.   ECCLESIASTES 11:6 NIV

Work shall be done for six days, but the seventh day shall be a holy day for you, a Sabbath of rest to the LORD.
EXODUS 35:2 NKJV

You should be strong. Don't give up, because you will get a reward for your good work.   2 CHRONICLES 15:7 NCV

May the favor of the Lord our God rest upon us; establish the work of our hands for us—yes, establish the work of our hands.
PSALM 90:17 NIV

Whatever your hand finds to do, do it with all your might.
ECCLESIASTES 9:10 NASB

Make it your goal to live a quiet life, minding your own business and working with your hands, just as we instructed you before. Then people who are not Christians will respect the way you live, and you will not need to depend on others.
1 THESSALONIANS 4:11–12 NLT

Observe people who are good at their work—
*   skilled workers are always in demand and admired;*
*   they don't take a backseat to anyone.*
PROVERBS 22:29 MSG

Today I Will Remember...

Have thy tools ready; God will find thee work.

CHARLES KINGSLEY

Do not pray for tasks equal to your powers. Pray for powers equal to your tasks. Then the doing of your work will be no miracle; but you shall be a miracle. PHILLIPS BROOKS

When man loses the sacred significance of work and of himself as a worker, he soon loses the sacred meaning of time and of life. CARL F. H. HENRY

If you feel that you are indispensable, put your finger in a glass of water, withdraw it, and note the hole you have left.

ANONYMOUS

God give me work till my life shall end and life till my work is done. WINIFRED HOLTBY

You spend more of your waking hours engaged in work than in any other activity. Can you imagine that your gracious heavenly Father... would want you to dread the largest slice of your life? Not a chance. ROBERT WOLGEMUTH

MONEY AND FINANCES

Trusting Enough to Prove God

Honor God with everything you own; give him the first and the best. PROVERBS 3:9 MSG

When the ancient Israelites were ready to enter the Promised Land, Moses had a long talk with them, sharing God's laws and lifestyle directives with the people. One of the first instructions God's people were to carry out when they got settled was to give something back to God. By giving back to God the Israelites would be reminded that God was the one who gives "the ability to produce wealth" (Deuteronomy 8:18 NIV). God also promised His people if they gave back to Him, He would bless them abundantly.

Fast forward several centuries to the 1970s. It was a time of recession in America. Money was tight. Layoffs were common. Every penny mattered because our family's income had been cut in half, yet the bills remained the same.

During this time a pastor at our church spoke about giving back to God. To my father this principle seemed unworkable, considering the times. Yet the minister reminded Dad that God had never canceled the idea of giving back. He suggested that Dad put God to the test for one month. Give back. See what happened. So that December, without telling anyone, Dad decided what he needed to do was put a tenth of everything he earned into the offering basket.

But as the end of the month drew near, so did the car payment. Because my father had been putting money in the church basket every week, it appeared he wouldn't have enough to make the payment. Dad said he had words with God about his

25

faithfulness in giving back to God. Yet the end of the month kept coming closer with no resolution to the money crunch in sight.

I, however, had known nothing about my father's test with God. Back in September I had decided to give Dad a practical Christmas gift. I had started saving my nickels and dimes and decided I'd give whatever I could save to Dad as his Christmas gift.

You can probably imagine the end of this story. When Dad opened my gift on Christmas morning, he dropped with a thump into his recliner. I had written a small note saying something about how I been saving to help out and hoped he'd be able to use the money. Don't you know the amount I had put into the envelope was exactly the amount my father was "short" to make the end-of-the-month car payment? And don't you know that from that December day until the day he died Dad never failed to give back to God again, for God had proved himself faithful?

When you're facing the tightened finances of unemployment it seems crazy to think about giving back to God. Unemployment checks aren't huge to begin with. And because giving back is not a magic formula that ensures God will perform for you in just the way you want Him to, there's no guarantee that your financial situation will be resolved in the same way that my father's situation was resolved. But know this for certain: God keeps His promises. " 'Test me in this,' says the LORD Almighty, 'and see if I will not throw open the floodgates of heaven and pour out so much blessing that you will not have room enough for it' " (Malachi 3:10 NIV). So will you trust God with your limited income? Try giving back and let God prove himself.

Getting Through Your Day

Remember that the LORD your God gives you the power to gain wealth, in order to confirm His covenant He swore to your fathers.   DEUTERONOMY 8:18 HCSB

Trust in your money and down you go! But the godly flourish like leaves in spring.   PROVERBS 11:28 NLT

Instruct those who are rich in this present world not to be conceited or to fix their hope on the uncertainty of riches, but on God, who richly supplies us with all things to enjoy.
                    1 TIMOTHY 6:17 NASB

Don't give me either poverty or riches. Feed me only the food I need, or I may feel satisfied and deny you and say, "Who is the Lord?"   PROVERBS 30:8–9 GOD'S WORD

Let no debt remain outstanding, except the continuing debt to love one another.   ROMANS 13:8 NIV

Whoever loves money will never have enough money; whoever loves wealth will not be satisfied with it.   ECCLESIASTES 5:10 NCV

Godliness with contentment is a great gain. For we brought nothing into the world, and we can take nothing out. But if we have food and clothing, we will be content with these. But those who want to be rich fall into temptation, a trap, and many foolish and harmful desires, which plunge people into ruin and destruction. For the love of money is a root of all kinds of evil, and by craving it, some have wandered away from the faith and pierced themselves with many pains.   1 TIMOTHY 6:6–10 HCSB

I know how to get along with humble means, and I also know how to live in prosperity; in any and every circumstance I have learned the secret of being filled and going hungry, both of having abundance and suffering need. PHILIPPIANS 4:12 NASB

Today I Will...

✓ Begin to give back to God a portion of whatever money, goods, or other income comes my way.

✓ Set up and follow a budget. I will keep it simple so I can stick with it, make sure it's livable, and review it often so that it can flex with life's changes.

✓ Track my expenses—every dollar used, even if it's for coffee. This will help me stay within my budget and help me make adjustments more quickly and not just spend on a whim.

✓ Save for emergencies. I will find a way to set aside a little each week to cover emergencies. (Suggestion: Put the money in a bank CD that will mature later when your income might be slimmer than it is now.)

✓ Renegotiate contracts if necessary. I will try to restructure my loans in ways that might be more helpful to me. (In Proverbs King Solomon suggests reviewing your contracts before those loans are called. Modern-day lenders would be willing to talk to you about this.)

✓ Be creative in making and saving money. I will try strategies like using online bill pay to save postage costs, using compact fluorescent light bulbs to use less energy, or having a yard sale with ridiculously low prices so I can make money and clean out overabundance.

✓ Make the tough decisions like selling my home, refusing to use my credit cards, putting off a new car lease or purchase for another year. I will make these choices knowing that these tough decisions will make each month easier for me and my family.

✓ Pray for God's guidance. I will search the Bible for God's attitude toward wealth and finances, knowing that I can survive a tough financial time by following God's plan and trusting Him to bring me through.

STRESS

Where Stress Can't Grow

The LORD spoke to Moses, saying, "Send men to spy out the land of Canaan, which I am giving to the children of Israel." NUMBERS 13:1–2 NKJV

If you're like most folks, you probably have a list of things you have to do today. (*Call the doctor. Walk the dog. Mow the lawn.*) It seems the more things you have on that list, the more pressure you feel to accomplish it all. (*Get the oil changed. Feed the fish. Return that call.*) When you blend in the physical, emotional, and mental strain of being unemployed or underemployed, you've found the master mix for stress. (*Check the e-mail. Take out the trash. Wash the dishes.*) It seems stress grows out of pressure situations without your realizing it.

Yet there's nothing really wrong with pressure, you know. Pressure keeps your tires inflated and wearing correctly. Pressure keeps the pistons moving in an engine. Pressure keeps the sails on a sailboat full of air so that the boat can be propelled forward. Pressure makes your favorite foods cook more quickly. Pressure is an okay thing. It's stress that's the killer.

The Israelites learned this lesson the hard way. When they stood on the outskirts of Canaan, God told Moses to assemble twelve men to go into the land that God was going to give them. God wanted the men to check out a few things. So Moses selected twelve leaders and gave them a "to do" list. While in the land of Canaan they were supposed to traverse the desert areas and climb up the hills. They had to assess the inhabitants of the land and determine their city sizes and fortifications. They were to consider the agricultural aspects of the land. Was the soil good? Were there trees on it? What did the crops look like? The list went on and on. Talk about pressure. It took the twelve men forty days to completely accomplish that list.

When the men returned to their families, the Bible says they told everyone how wonderful the land was. In fact they brought back a bunch of grapes that was so large it took two men to carry it. The Israelites were encouraged. The pressure of moving to this new land seemed doable.

But then ten of the men allowed negative thoughts to darken their counsel. In a matter of moments the crowd went from hopeful to fearful. Despite Joshua and Caleb's urging to trust God and rely on His promises, the negative words spawned such stress that the people began to weep and wail. Their slide into stress ended up eventually killing every last one of them over the next forty years. Joshua and Caleb escaped that death sentence, however, because they refused to focus on the negative. They trusted God and kept their hearts centered on Him, on His truth, on His promises, and on His words. God, in return, granted them long life and great blessing.

Pressure is inevitable when riding the roller coaster of unemployment. Yet you can keep pressure from becoming stress by trusting God and not focusing on the negatives, just like Joshua and Caleb. The apostle Paul adds that you should think only about things that are right, noble, true, pure, lovely, excellent, admirable, and praiseworthy. Remind yourself of these truths, of God's love for you, of His promises to care for you. You'll find stress will have a hard time growing in the soil of such trust and truth.

Getting Through Your Day

Jesus said, "Come to me, all of you who are weary and carry heavy burdens, and I will give you rest. Take my yoke upon you. Let me teach you, because I am humble and gentle at heart, and you will find rest for your souls. For my yoke is easy to bear, and the burden I give you is light."   MATTHEW 11:28–30 NLT

In my distress I called to the LORD; I called out to my God. From his temple he heard my voice; my cry came to his ears.

2 SAMUEL 22:7 NIV

He gives strength to the weary and strengthens the powerless. Youths may faint and grow weary, and young men stumble and fall, but those who trust in the LORD will renew their strength; they will soar on wings like eagles; they will run and not grow weary; they will walk and not faint.   ISAIAH 40:29–31 HCSB

I will give rest and strength to those who are weak and tired.

JEREMIAH 31:25 NCV

The LORD is my shepherd; I shall not want. He makes me to lie down in green pastures; He leads me beside the still waters. He restores my soul; He leads me in the paths of righteousness for His name's sake.   PSALM 23:1–3 NKJV

Then Jesus said, "Let's go off by ourselves to a quiet place and rest awhile." He said this because there were so many people coming and going that Jesus and his apostles didn't even have time to eat.   MARK 6:31 NLT

[Jesus said,] "Do not let your hearts be troubled. Trust in God; trust also in me."   JOHN 14:1 NIV

Today I Will Pray For...

✓ A clear perspective. If I stand at the foot of the mountains, they seem impassable. If I fly over them in an airliner, their heights appear attainable. Impassable or attainable—it's all a matter of perspective.

✓ A sense of joy. Joy releases my inner creativity, whereas stress squelches it. Though facing the stress of debtor's prison, George Frideric Handel found joy through the creativity of composing *Messiah*.

✓ A kind spirit. Some people have a tendency to lash out with harsh words or actions when under stress. I will make it a point to strive for a kind, gentle spirit when under stress.

✓ Integrity. When under stress it's easier to be less than truthful on a resume. To reduce stress, I will be principled in my dealings. I'll have less to apologize for later.

✓ Strength. I'm not the only one on the planet going through a tough time right now, but there are days when it feels like it. I will ask God to show me how to escape stress and replace it with His strength.

✓ God's grace to fill me today. I need His Holy Spirit to flow freely through my life and my dealings with others so that I can be free from the paralyzing grip of stress.

PERSONALIZE THE RIDE

As you climb the heights and begin your ride, use this space to clarify and record your thoughts. Writing things down can help relieve pressure and be a good reminder of your thoughts and actions later on. Here are a few questions to get you started. Answer as few or as many of them as you like.

- How do I feel today? (Remember, the only bad feelings are the ones you stuff down inside.)
- What do I want God to know today? (Be honest; He knows how you feel anyway.)
- What am I facing today? (Be specific with what is on your plate.)
- What should I do? (Is there an action you can take?)
- I am thankful today for... (There is always something to thank God for!)

2

WHOOSHING DOWN THE HILL

How did you do when you were on the employment ride—when you were on the roller coaster of work? Were you comfortable in your seat? Happy with the other riders in your roller-coaster car? Thrilled to be climbing and moving forward? When you were working, you probably felt that way some of the time.

How did you feel when you came to the top of that long hill, when the tracks of the employment ride were no longer visible? How did you feel when you saw the pink slip in your pay envelope, had that talk with the personnel director, or heard your boss say you were no longer needed? That's when the roller-coaster car of work teetered on the summit, slipped over the edge, whooshed down the hill, and dragged you along with it. That's when you went from employed to unemployed, and there wasn't a thing you could do about it.

Most roller-coaster enthusiasts enjoy all the aspects of those thrill rides. To roller-coaster buffs, that long climb up the first hill can be boring. There's nothing better to these folks than that first stomach-lurching sense of free-fall into nothingness. However, there's a picture in my memory of a friend who loves roller-coaster rides who happened to be looking toward the rear of the car at the exact moment the coaster slipped over the summit. Facing rearward left him totally unprepared for the plummet, and he had such a look of horror on his face!

When you lost your job, you probably felt like my friend did. Whether your job loss was unexpected or something you saw coming, the freefall was still pretty horrifying, a drop-kick to the stomach that left you heaving. What follows in its place is a sense that what's coming next isn't going to be pretty, either. You've fallen down the hill, and everything is moving so fast you can't catch your breath.

While you'd prefer to climb the heights of job success without interruption, job loss can happen. But whether you're experiencing good times or bad, the Bible says God is still faithful. He is still kind and loving. He is bigger than any trouble that might overtake you. And He has promised to care for you. Those are all valuable lessons to remember as you ride this unemployment ride. There are a few things you can do to make this ride easier as well.

My rearward-facing coaster friend knew that continuing to face rearward as he rode the roller coaster would only make his journey worse. It's the same for you. Whether you like it or not, you're on a ride that's going forward. By facing backwards and dwelling on the past, on what just happened to your old job, on what you've lost and left behind, you won't be able to move forward on this unemployment ride. To successfully ride this roller coaster of unemployment, you need to be prepared for what's coming. You have to deal with the feelings, situations, circumstances, and needs that have tumbled into the coaster car with you as you've whooshed down that first hill. As you face forward for the remainder of the ride, take time for a head-on look at what God has to say about failure, loss, fear, prayer, and assurance.

FAILURE

Peter and the Rooster

We are hard pressed on every side, but not crushed;
perplexed, but not in despair; persecuted, but not abandoned;
struck down, but not destroyed. 2 CORINTHIANS 4:8–9 NIV

Don't count on me to make a perfect centerpiece for a fancy dinner table. Martha Stewart I'm not. Don't ask me to participate in your telephone campaign to raise funds for some worthy cause. I have the telephone personality of a dead fish. It's true. I know me, and I'm a total failure when it comes to some things.

But I didn't think I'd be a failure at work. After all, anyone can hold down a job, right? My mind tells me it's only losers who can't stay employed, only failures who can't bring home a paycheck. An inner judgmental attitude beats me up and says, "You could have done more... *should* have done more. If you had, then your job wouldn't have been cut. Now you're a big fat zero, just like your nonexistent paycheck." At least that's how it feels.

If you're struggling because you've lost a job, you might feel something similar. You might be judging yourself for your shortcomings, inabilities, or your failure to keep your job. Yet the sense of failure is an honest emotion and a true reaction all folks go through when they've put their heart and time into something and it doesn't work out the way they had hoped.

Consider the Bible story of Peter and the rooster. Jesus and His disciples were sharing supper when Jesus said He was going away and that His friends could not go with Him. Peter impetuously protested, declaring he wanted to go wherever Jesus went. He said he'd even die for Jesus.

Because Jesus knew what was about to happen, because He knew Peter better than Peter knew himself, Jesus asked him if he really meant what he'd just said. Then Jesus told Peter some shocking news. "Before the rooster crows," He said, "you will disown me three times!" (John 13:38 NIV). Talk about failure. To be in front of all your friends and have Jesus announce that you're going to do something shameful before the night was over. That's true failure!

Yet do you know what Jesus said next? Jesus didn't condemn Peter for his impending failure. He didn't judge him or tell him how disappointed He'd be in him. Rather, Jesus wanted Peter to know that even though He knew the future, even though He knew Peter would fail miserably, nothing could change the fact that Jesus loved him. Failure or not—it didn't matter. Nothing Peter could do would make Jesus love him any less. Jesus went right to the heart of Peter's failure and said, "Do not let your hearts be troubled. Trust in God" (John 14:1 NIV).

Instead of hammering judgment onto Peter's failure, Jesus offered him comfort. You see, while comfort is the last thing you expect to find in the face of failure, comfort is the first thing God offers. There will be times in your life you will fail at things, just like Peter did. Sometimes those failures will be huge, too. Yet God longs to comfort you, just as He comforted Peter. Hear God say to you, "Take comfort. Trust me to be the God you've known me to be. I know you. I know what you're going to do, and I love you anyway. You're not a failure to me. Don't let your heart be troubled. Trust me."

Getting Through Your Day

Our enemies have no reason to gloat over us. We have fallen, but we will rise again. We are in darkness now, but the LORD will give us light.
                                                        MICAH 7:8 GNT

I said, "I have worked hard for nothing. I have used my strength, but I didn't accomplish anything. Yet, certainly my case is in the Lord's hands, and my reward is with my God."

ISAIAH 49:4 GOD'S WORD

The Lord directs the steps of the godly. He delights in every detail of their lives. Though they stumble, they will never fall, for the Lord holds them by the hand. PSALM 37:23–24 NLT

If we are faithless, he remains faithful—for he cannot deny himself. 2 TIMOTHY 2:13 ESV

We know that God causes all things to work together for good to those who love God, to those who are called according to His purpose. ROMANS 8:28 NASB

Everyone who hears these words of mine and puts them into practice is like a wise man who built his house on the rock. The rain came down, the streams rose, and the winds blew and beat against that house; yet it did not fall, because it had its foundation on the rock. But everyone who hears these words of mine and does not put them into practice is like a foolish man who built his house on sand. The rain came down, the streams rose, and the winds blew and beat against that house, and it fell with a great crash. MATTHEW 7:24–27 NIV

Today I Will...

✓ Be comforted by God in the midst of my job situation. Whether underemployed or unemployed, I choose to listen to the words of Jesus and trust God to take care of my situation.

✓ Talk to a trusted friend about my job loss and the sense of failure I feel in that job loss. And I will ask that friend to pray for me.

✓ Discard the feeling of failure and replace it with an attitude of expectancy for the new job that God is already bringing my way.

✓ Remember the failure of Peter as well as the successes that followed in his life, knowing that this failure and job loss in my life can lead to better days ahead for me, too.

✓ Seek the advice of a job counselor to help me polish my resume and talk through new options for job possibilities.

✓ Ask God to show me if my failure in my last job was due to any wrongdoing, poor attitude, or personal reason I may need to correct. I will trust Him to show me if I need to clear the air with anyone.

FEAR

Just Like Eagles

Those who trust in the LORD will find new strength. They will
soar high on wings like eagles. They will run and not grow weary.
They will walk and not faint. ISAIAH 40:31 NLT

I once lived along the Mississippi River not far from one of
its locks and dams. Several families of bald eagles made their
homes in the trees that grew along the riverside levees. In the
winter these eagles would fly over the dam, swooping down to
snatch fish from the river. Every spring when the trees were in
full bloom, you could see baby eaglets in their nests. The parents were kept busy bringing food to the little ones.

But then in late spring, just when those baby eaglets were
getting comfortable in that nest, the mother bird would begin
to behave strangely. She'd start ripping the nest apart in an
effort to get the eaglets out of their comfort zone and into the
air. After all, eagles are made to fly, not to sit in nests. If the
mother eagle didn't tear up the nest, the babies would never
learn to fly.

As the nest would get smaller, the eaglets would holler
and make an awful racket because they were afraid. Yet the
mother eagle was vigilant. If one of the little ones fell out of
what remained of the nest she would call to it, probably yelling
instructions on how to stretch out a wing or ride on an air current. If the little one didn't comply, the mother eagle quickly
swooped down under the falling eaglet. She'd catch it on her
body and bring it back to the top of the tree. She'd keep this
process up, too, until the nest was completely destroyed and all
her children had learned to fly on their own.

41

Ever feel like a fearful baby eaglet? It's human nature to fear. In some instances fear is a good thing. For example, the fear of falling through thin ice can keep you from walking out onto it. But debilitating fear that paralyzes you and keeps you from moving forward is not a good fear.

Unfortunately, such paralyzing fear can accompany a job loss. You're afraid of going this way because you don't know what awaits you. You're afraid of going the other way because you might miss out on something needful. You're afraid of how long this will last and how you'll cope. The upheavals and uncertainties of what will happen next seem to threaten your existence. Your nest of job security is all torn up.

In essence you're a lot like the baby eaglets. Yet the Bible says God is more vigilant than a mother eagle. Just when you think you'll hit rock bottom from that unemployment fall, here comes the Lord, swooping in to catch you and lift you to safety. He'll do it every time, too, for Isaiah says: "In his love and mercy he redeemed them; he lifted them up and carried them all the days of old" (Isaiah 63:9 NIV).

Sometimes it's hard not to be afraid. God knows this. But remember the baby eagles. They had to leave the nest for their own good, but they were never at risk because their momma was watching. And you're never at risk either, for God is more watchful than that momma eagle. Ask God to help you replace your fear of the unknown with a deeper trust in His keeping hand. Then you'll be ready to fly on wings, just like eagles.

Getting Through Your Day

The LORD is my light and my salvation; whom shall I fear? The LORD is the stronghold of my life; of whom shall I be afraid?

PSALM 27:1 ESV

42

What is the price of five sparrows—two copper coins? Yet God does not forget a single one of them. And the very hairs on your head are all numbered. So don't be afraid; you are more valuable to God than a whole flock of sparrows.   LUKE 12:6–7 NLT

You drew near when I called on You; You said, "Do not fear!" O Lord, You have pleaded my soul's cause; You have redeemed my life.   LAMENTATIONS 3:57–58 NASB

God is our protection and our strength. He always helps in times of trouble. So we will not be afraid even if the earth shakes, or the mountains fall into the sea, even if the oceans roar and foam, or the mountains shake at the raging sea.   PSALM 46:1–3 NCV

Even when I am afraid, I still trust you. I praise the word of God. I trust God. I am not afraid. What can mere flesh and blood do to me?   PSALM 56:3–4 GOD'S WORD

Do not fear, for I am with you; do not be dismayed, for I am your God. I will strengthen you and help you; I will uphold you with my righteous right hand.   ISAIAH 41:10 NIV

The Spirit that God has given you does not make you slaves and cause you to be afraid; instead, the Spirit makes you God's children, and by the Spirit's power we cry out to God, "Father! my Father!"   ROMANS 8:15 GNT

Today I Will Pray...

✓ For a willingness to release my fear to God. Sometimes I hold onto fear because it's more comfortable than the unknown. But God doesn't want me paralyzed by fear. I will release it in prayer.

✓ For a greater trust in God's love for me. The Bible says, "There is no fear in love. But perfect love drives out fear" (1 John 4:18 NIV). By trusting God's love for me, fear won't find an easy foothold in my life.

✓ For a renewed concern for others. When I turn my eyes and focus on others and their needs, even if only for a little bit, I'll find my own fears will lessen.

✓ For a renewed memory. Recalling when God has helped me through tough times in the past is a great way to send fear running. God is just as able to help me now as He did then.

✓ Scripture back to God. As I face fearful days, I will pray Psalm 86 aloud. I could also write this psalm in a notebook or prayer journal. As I pray these verses and believe these words, I'll find fear will flee.

LOSS

My Prayer Today

*God blesses you who weep now, for in due time
you will laugh.*   LUKE 6:21 NLT

Dear Lord,

I just feel sad inside. I find myself sitting and staring into space. I know it was only a job. It's not like a person died or anything, but this hurts. It feels like my life has come to an end somehow. Some days I can't believe it's real. I pinch myself to try and wake up from this awful nightmare but find it isn't a dream. It's a new, sick reality. And it's all mine.

Then some days I get so angry and resentful. Why me? Why not someone else? Why now? I've been good. I didn't do anything wrong. Why am I being punished? It's just not fair!

And then, Lord, I get sick and tired of twirling on that emotional roller coaster. So I square my shoulders and decide to be strong and tough. I won't let any of this bother me any more. I don't need that old job anyway. I'm bigger than they are. I'm better than that. They don't know how much they lost when they lost me.

But then the next day dawns, and Lord, I'm still here. I still don't have a job. I'm scared, discouraged, overwhelmed. I don't know what to do . . . so I sit . . . and stare out the window . . .

Is this what they call grief, Lord? I thought grief only happened when people died. But then I guess I've experienced a loss of my own—the loss of my job—and the loss of the dream I had that was attached to my job—that American dream of security and success, that biblical dream of blessing and abundance. Now I stare into a hole as dark as a freshly dug grave.

My emotions are all over the map, and I'm having a hard time moving past this. Lord, I need your help. I can't handle this sense of loss alone. This job loss, this upheaval in my life, has become a priority to me. So Lord, my prayer today is, would you please make my loss your priority too?

I know you understand sorrow and loss because you experienced grief. After all, the shortest verse in the Bible says "Jesus wept." You lost friends and loved ones, Lord. You grieved for the nation of Israel because her people didn't recognize you as the Savior of the world. I find comfort in knowing that you felt these feelings of loss and grief. That means you *do* know how I feel, Lord. You've been here before. And that helps.

Ecclesiastes 3 says there is a time for everything, including a time to weep and a time to laugh, a time to mourn and a time to dance. Lord, this is my time to mourn, to weep over the loss of my job. This is my time of grief. I know I need to get through this in order to heal, in order to be stronger on the other side of this loss. So thank you for the reminder that it's all right for me to feel sad about losing my job. Thank you for the assurance that you'll be with me through this reorganizing of my life. Thank you that you've said even though I'm weeping now, one day I'll laugh again. I give it all to you, Lord. Thanks for your faithfulness. And thanks for listening and understanding, too.

Getting Through Your Day

Everything has its own time, and there is a specific time for every activity under heaven: a time to be born and a time to die, a time to plant and a time to pull out what was planted, a time to kill and a time to heal, a time to tear down and a time to build up, a time to cry and a time to laugh, a time to mourn and a time to dance, a time to scatter stones and a time to gather them.

ECCLESIASTES 3:1–5 GOD'S WORD

You're blessed when you're at the end of your rope. With less of you there is more of God and his rule. You're blessed when you feel you've lost what is most dear to you. Only then can you be embraced by the One most dear to you.   MATTHEW 5:3–4 MSG

For men are not cast off by the Lord forever. Though he brings grief, he will show compassion, so great is his unfailing love. For he does not willingly bring affliction or grief to the children of men.   LAMENTATIONS 3:31–33 NIV

As we share abundantly in Christ's sufferings, so through Christ we share abundantly in comfort too. If we are afflicted, it is for your comfort and salvation; and if we are comforted, it is for your comfort, which you experience when you patiently endure the same sufferings that we suffer.   2 CORINTHIANS 1:5–6 ESV

Heavens and earth, be happy. Mountains, shout with joy, because the Lord comforts his people and will have pity on those who suffer.   ISAIAH 49:13 NCV

[Because of] the LORD's faithful love we do not perish, for His mercies never end. They are new every morning; great is Your faithfulness!   LAMENTATIONS 3:22–23 HCSB

Today I Will Remember...

Jesus Christ's life was an absolute failure from every standpoint but God's.   OSWALD CHAMBERS

The human soul, beaten down, overwhelmed, faced by complete failure and ruin, can still rise up against unbearable odds and triumph.   HAROLD RUSSELL

When you feel that all is lost, sometimes the greatest gain is ready to be yours.   THOMAS À KEMPIS

It is a wonder what God can do with a broken heart, if He gets all the pieces.   SAMUEL CHADWICK

God sometimes washes the eyes of his children with tears in order that they may read aright his providence.

THEODORE LEDYARD CUYLER

God whispers in our pleasures but shouts in our pain.

C. S. LEWIS

PRAYER

Ask First

*Jesus went up a hill to pray and spent the whole night there
praying to God. When day came, he called his disciples to
him and chose twelve of them.*   LUKE 6:12–13 GNT

Have you ever heard the old adage, God helps those who help
themselves? I did. Lots of times. In fact I was taught this was
the reason I had to be self-sufficient. I was supposed to help
God out by learning to tie my own shoes, make my bed, cook
my meals, and do my laundry.

But did you know that this old adage runs contrary to the
Bible? The Bible says God helps each of His children, including those who *cannot* help themselves. Nowhere does the Bible
urge God's children to stand on their own or be self-reliant
without His Spirit to direct them. God's kids are supposed to
depend on Him for guidance and direction, provision and protection. They are to stay in constant contact with Him, too, so
that they will go, do, and say what He wants. The only way
to stay in such contact is to pray, and pray often. The Bible
adds that those who rely only on themselves do so at their own
peril.

When the ancient Israelites were settling the Promised
Land, God instructed them to take over certain cities that
worshiped idols. Joshua and his soldiers had already successfully attacked Jericho and Ai. The people of Gibeon knew they
would soon be attacked too, so they dressed several men in
rags. They gave them moldy bread and worn-out wineskins
and sent them to Joshua. These men lied and said they lived far
away. They wanted a peace treaty with the Israelites because

they claimed they were poor and Israel was strong. Unfortunately the Israelites "did not inquire of the LORD" (Joshua 9:14 NIV). They relied on their own brains and ability and granted the liars' request. Thus Israel made peace with an enemy God had told them to destroy because they neglected to pray about their decision first. From then on the Gibeonites' idolatrous ways were a serious problem for God's people.

Jesus, on the other hand, "often withdrew to lonely places and prayed" (Luke 5:16 NIV). Jesus, God's Son, a person who rightly could have been self-sufficient, who could have relied on His own brains and ability to make His decisions, didn't do so. And Luke 6:12–13 tells us that before He chose the men who would be His twelve disciples, Jesus spent the whole night in prayer. He didn't rely on His own instinct. Instead Jesus prayed to make sure He and God the Father were of one mind. Before He did anything, Jesus asked first.

Which example have you been following? Are you relying on your own strength, brainpower, and networking skills to get through each day? To successfully survive unemployment you need to be less self-reliant (like Joshua) and more God-reliant (like Jesus). Go ahead and wash the dishes, do the laundry, and make your bed by yourself, but when it comes to making a decision or choosing where to apply for work, ask God first. Trust Him to help you, even if you could help yourself, and especially when you can't, for God stands ready to help. So ask first, and ask often. Remember, many vital decisions are recorded in the Bible, yet the ones that were ultimately successful were the ones preceded by much prayer.

So ... have you prayed like Jesus today?

Getting Through Your Day

Before they call out, I'll answer. Before they've finished speaking, I'll have heard.   ISAIAH 65:24 MSG

Ask, and it will be given to you; seek, and you will find; knock, and it will be opened to you. For everyone who asks receives, and he who seeks finds, and to him who knocks it will be opened.
                                                        MATTHEW 7:7–8 NASB

Open your ears to my prayer, O LORD. Pay attention when I plead for mercy. When I am in trouble, I call out to you because you answer me.   PSALM 86:6–7 GOD'S WORD

Call to Me and I will answer you and tell you great and wondrous things you do not know.   JEREMIAH 33:3 HCSB

Pray to the LORD for the city where you are living, because if good things happen in the city, good things will happen to you also.
                                                        JEREMIAH 29:7 NCV

The Lord watches over the righteous and listens to their prayers; but he opposes those who do evil.   1 PETER 3:12 GNT

Today I Will Get This Off My Chest...

Use the space below to respond to as few or as many of these questions as you like.

- Do you have a daily appointment time with God? Do you keep that commitment? Why or why not?
- It has been said that those who pray most, accomplish most; those who pray a little, accomplish a little;

but those who don't pray and rely only on self, don't accomplish anything. Do you believe this to be true? Why or why not?

- How can you better follow Jesus' example to withdraw often to pray? How would a continual life of conversation with God—praying without ceasing—look in the actual working out of your daily life?

- Do you always remember to ask God first about your employment decisions? Or are you a believer in "God only helps those who help themselves"? How should prayer affect your career transition time?

ASSURANCE

This Is for You

There has never been the slightest doubt in my mind that the God who started this great work in you would keep at it and bring it to a flourishing finish. PHILIPPIANS 1:6 MSG

I hadn't worked in almost six months when my husband received the news he wasn't needed at his workplace any more either. Do you know what that means for my household? Now there were two adults of the three who occupy our home who had no visible means of support. Welcome to my world.

I've been here before. I've ridden this roller coaster of unemployment more times than I care to count. Yet a wise friend once reminded me that heaven's angels weren't wringing their hands because we were once again without work. They weren't crying, "How did this get past God? Didn't He notice what was happening?" The same friend assured me that God was aware of my situation, that He cared, and that God was working to bring about His best plan for my life.

However, when days go by without a reply to e-mails, a response to a resume, or a return of a phone call, the gnawing question "Are you really doing anything, Lord?" surfaces. It attaches to the brain and tries to worm its way into your heart. And that's where I found myself one morning not long ago as I headed out to church.

So I prayed.

I told the Lord I was scared. I said it would be helpful if He could reassure me in some way that He had everything in control. And, I added, if God had to change the pastor's message just so I'd know, I'd sure appreciate it.

I'll admit I was barely paying attention when the preacher finally began to speak. But all that changed when he said, "I had a sermon all prepared, but the Lord laid another message on my heart this morning." Had I heard him right? The Lord had told him to change his sermon?

Then the pastor started to read from Matthew 14:22–31, and I started to cry. Why? Unbeknownst to him, this was the same Bible passage another pastor had preached on when my husband had lost his job back in 1992. In this passage, Peter starts to walk to Jesus across the water but gets scared by the storm. He starts to sink and hollers, "Lord, save me!" The Bible says, "Immediately Jesus reached out his hand and caught him" (Matthew 14:31 NIV). Back in 1992 I had been just as scared as Peter and had called out for God's help. Now here we were facing the storm of unemployment again. I had needed God's reassurance once more, had prayed for help, and God had answered with Matthew 14.

I'll confess I didn't pay a whole lot of attention to the sermon because I was so overwhelmed by God's response. It was as if He stood right beside me and said, "This is for you." Indeed, only God could have arranged that sermon choice. It may seem like a small thing, but it was the assurance I needed, the reminder that God is aware, He is in control, and He will do exceedingly, abundantly more than we can ever ask or imagine. That assurance is yours, too. Pray. Ask. Holler for help. And God will provide the assurance you need in just the way you need it.

Getting Through Your Day

It is God himself who has set us apart, who has placed his mark of ownership upon us, and who has given us the Holy Spirit in our hearts as the guarantee of all that he has in store for us.

2 CORINTHIANS 1:21–22 GNT

54

Though I walk in the midst of trouble, You will revive me; You will stretch forth Your hand against the wrath of my enemies, and Your right hand will save me. The LORD will accomplish what concerns me; Your lovingkindness, O LORD, is everlasting.

PSALM 138:7–8 NASB

I will be glad and rejoice in your love, because you saw my suffering; you knew my troubles. You have not handed me over to my enemies but have set me in a safe place.   PSALM 31:7–8 NCV

We do not have a high priest who is unable to sympathize with our weaknesses, but we have one who has been tempted in every way, just as we are—yet was without sin. Let us then approach the throne of grace with confidence, so that we may receive mercy and find grace to help us in our time of need.   HEBREWS 4:15–16 NIV

All praise to the God and Father of our Master, Jesus the Messiah! Father of all mercy! God of all healing counsel! He comes alongside us when we go through hard times, and before you know it, he brings us alongside someone else who is going through hard times so that we can be there for that person just as God was there for us.   2 CORINTHIANS 1:3–4 MSG

Give all your worries and cares to God, for he cares about you.

1 PETER 5:7 NLT

Today I Will...

✓ Be thankful that Jesus Christ is able to sympathize with every need and every concern that I have.
✓ Be grateful for the promises in God's Word that He loves me, that He has a wonderful plan for my life, and that He will fulfill His purpose for me.

✓ Appreciate the friends and family who pray for me and remind me of God's faithfulnesses in my life.

✓ Be pleased to remember that God is able to do, and is doing, more than I can even imagine.

✓ Be glad about the access I have in prayer to come to God's throne and leave my cares at His feet, knowing He will work everything out in His time.

✓ Learn a valuable lesson from the example of Peter, who, as he was sinking under the waves, called out for help. Jesus came immediately to his aid. The assurance of Jesus' help is mine, too, for the Lord has promised good to me.

PERSONALIZE THE RIDE

Use this space to clarify and record your thoughts about your ride. Consider what you've read about failure, fear, loss, prayer, and assurance as you respond to as many or as few of these honest questions as you like:

- What is your greatest fear? What needs to change in your life so that you can trust God to overcome this?
- What should you pray about today? Are you holding on to past hurts, failures, or losses?
- What do you want God to know today? How is today different from yesterday?
- What should you do? Is there an action you can take that you haven't taken yet? (Suggestion: Write a list of all your concerns and leave them on this page for God to handle.)
- I am thankful today for... (There is always something to be grateful to God for.)

3

Loop THE Loop

I can still remember it. The Dragon Coaster looked so exciting in that television commercial. The announcer animatedly hyped the thrill of the entire ride, but what really caught my eye was the loop-the-loop section. The steel roller-coaster frame was painted a lustrous grass-green with forest-green track segments twining around it. The advertisement showed smiling riders seamlessly moving from upright to upside down and back again with ease. When I arrived at the amusement park and finally saw the Dragon Coaster in person, I realized the advertisement was spot on. Driven by the velocity it gained from the first drop, the roller-coaster car and its riders flew through that loop section without a hesitation. With a loud roaring, whooshing zoom it was gone. The Dragon Coaster riders were in that loop-the-loop for mere seconds, but wow! What a ride!

In like fashion, the roller-coaster ride of unemployment has its own loop-the-loop segment. The speed at which your life changed when you lost your job rivals the speed of a roller-coaster car as it plummets down its first big hill. But then, just as you begin to grasp the reality of the unemployment ride, you find yourself twisted and whirled about emotionally, spiritually, and personally, just like roller-coaster riders are twirled about in the loop-the-loop. Sometimes it seems you're right side up and handling things okay, but in mere moments you can find yourself upside down, topsy-turvy, all twisted up inside. Your emotions are all over the place—up and positive one moment, but then bitter, angry, and depressed the next. One day you'll feel close to God and sure of His care in your life, but before the day is over you'll probably be fighting back fear, questioning whether God is even aware of your situation, or, if He is, if He is the one wreaking this havoc on your life in the first place.

The unemployment ride brings every rider to this point. But there's one major thing to remember about the loop-the-loop time—it doesn't last forever. If you'd look at an amusement park roller-coaster ride from a bird's-eye view, you'd see that the loop section of the thrill ride takes up very little space in the overall length of the entire ride. The actual time a roller-coaster rider spends in the vortex of the loop is one of the shortest moments of the ride. It's the same for your unemployment ride. This loop-the-loop time is a tough one, but the wonderful message is, it won't last forever.

The Bible acknowledges that hard times won't last forever either. More than 170 times in the Old Testament you'll find the phrase "it came to pass." When you're going round and round with the whirling pressures of the vortex of unemployment, it's heartening to hear the words "it came to *pass*." God alone knows how long anything will last, but you can let this oft-repeated phrase from Scripture bring you hope that your time of unemployment will also "come to pass." You won't be in this situation forever. This loop-the-loop time on your unemployment ride will pass for you more quickly if you deal with a few issues like anger, discouragement, God's sovereignty, faith, and your words.

ANGER

Do You Want to Get Well?

*Jesus saw him lying there, and he knew that the man
had been sick for such a long time; so he asked him,
"Do you want to get well?"*   JOHN 5:6 GNT

The Bible tells the story of a man who had been crippled for
thirty-eight years. This man spent his days at the Pool of
Bethesda in Jerusalem. Waiting for a miracle, the blind, sick,
lame, and paralyzed would come and lie on porches that sur-
rounded the pool. According to the Bible an angel would come
occasionally and stir the pool water. "Then whoever stepped in
first, after the stirring of the water, was made well of whatever
disease he had" (John 5:4 NKJV).

One day when Jesus went to Jerusalem, He happened to
pass this pool and noticed this crippled man. The Bible says
Jesus could tell that this man had been an invalid for a long
time. He spoke to the man and asked him, "Do you want to
get well?"

Strange question, don't you think? Why wouldn't the fellow have wanted to get well? Here he was, lying next to the
only place in town that had a reputation for healing. Here he
was, wasting away in front of every person who passed by.
Who in his right mind wouldn't want to be healed of this crip-
pling infirmity? Who, indeed?

Me, for one. At least for a few days last week when I was
crippled. Not paralyzed in my arms or legs, but paralyzed by
anger and bitterness at the fellow who had made the decision
to issue my pink slip. I was so resentful that he had put me
on this roller coaster of unemployment; if I had had him in

earshot I would have let him have it. As it was, God heard my anger-crippling outburst. I put on a holier-than-thou attitude that probably disgusted God, praying that He would protect this terrible boss from the ravages of joblessness so he wouldn't have to go through all the ups and downs and closed doors that I had been facing. I prayed mightily in my self-righteousness that God wouldn't let that rotten fellow hear the same down-sizing speech I had heard. And then in my tirade I heard the soft voice of Jesus say, "Do you want to get well?"

The mental image of a thirty-eight-year invalid atrophying alongside a place of healing knocked the wind out of me, for that's what I was becoming. I was becoming an invalid of anger. Resentment was wasting my spirit away. Bitterness was consuming my heart. Anger was so easy to hold onto, much easier than struggling toward a pool for the healing water of forgiveness, understanding, or grace.

When Jesus asked the crippled man if he wanted to get well, the man said yes. Problem was, he had been crippled for too long. He couldn't get down to the pool fast enough to be the first person into the water to get healed.

So do you know what Jesus did? Jesus said to the man, "Get up. Pick up your mat. Walk." And the Bible says the man did just that.

When anger, resentment, and bitterness grasp and clutch at your heart, Jesus' question makes sense. Do you want to get well? Do you want to give up the shriveling, wasting away, withering effect that anger and its kinfolk produce? Do you want to get well? The man said yes, and he was immediately healed. What will your answer be?

Getting Through Your Day

Beloved, never avenge yourselves, but leave it to the wrath of God, for it is written, "Vengeance is mine, I will repay, says the Lord."   ROMANS 12:19 ESV

A gentle answer turns away wrath, but a harsh word stirs up anger.   PROVERBS 15:1 NIV

When you are angry, do not sin, and be sure to stop being angry before the end of the day. Do not give the devil a way to defeat you.   EPHESIANS 4:26–27 NCV

Everyone must be quick to hear, slow to speak and slow to anger; for the anger of man does not achieve the righteousness of God.   JAMES 1:19–20 NASB

Don't be quick to fly off the handle. Anger boomerangs. You can spot a fool by the lumps on his head.   ECCLESIASTES 7:9 MSG

Love is patient. Love is kind. Love isn't jealous. It doesn't sing its own praises. It isn't arrogant. It isn't rude. It doesn't think about itself. It isn't irritable. It doesn't keep track of wrongs.
1 CORINTHIANS 13:4–5 GOD'S WORD

I tell you that anyone who is angry with his brother will be subject to judgment… Therefore, if you are offering your gift at the altar and there remember that your brother has something against you, leave your gift there in front of the altar. First go and be reconciled to your brother; then come and offer your gift.
MATTHEW 5:22–24 NIV

Today I Will Pray...

✓ That God will show me any situations in my life where I harbor anger or resentment. As God reveals these things to me, I will ask His forgiveness for each offense.

✓ For the ability to look beyond my hurt and to recognize people who might be angry with me. I will seek God's wisdom to know what to do to restore these broken relationships.

✓ For God's touch on my life to shine a spotlight on any unforgiveness I might be holding against someone that I have been angry or resentful toward.

✓ And honestly share my feelings of anger at God for the way He is working in my life right now—how everything feels unfair, that it seems He's inactive, that things are resolving way too slowly. And I will ask God's forgiveness for my anger toward Him.

✓ For God's help when I am tempted to get angry and that He will fill me with His Holy Spirit and grant me self-control. I will prayerfully look for God's perspective on the situation.

✓ For those I have been angry toward and genuinely ask God to bless them with good things, wisdom, and a clear sense of His presence with them, knowing that such a heart attitude will release me from the withering effects of pent-up resentment.

DISCOURAGEMENT

Hiding and Hurting

I have been very zealous for the LORD God of Hosts, but the Israelites have abandoned Your covenant, torn down Your altars, and killed Your prophets with the sword. I alone am left, and they are looking for me to take my life. 1 KINGS 19:10 HCSB

My husband Mike groaned as we talked together over a cup of coffee. "I've never been penniless before," he said. "Light on cash, sure. Waiting till Friday for the paycheck, definitely. But never just flat, busted broke with no income, no money coming from anywhere, and bills to pay. I'm so beaten and discouraged I don't know where to turn."

As a Christian, Mike is certain of God's love for him. He is confident that God is aware of his situation. He has lost jobs before, but during those times there had always been work readily available in his field of expertise. This time it's different. Hundreds of qualified applicants compete for only a few job openings. And like everyone else who can't find work, Mike fights a battle with discouragement. Without a job, the pressures of family, rising costs, and bills pile up. It's hard to find encouragement amidst the dismal odds. In effect Mike feels a lot like Elijah.

The prophet Elijah spoke for God during a difficult time in the life of Israel. Following the example of their kings, the Israelites had abandoned God's ways. They had begun to worship idols and actively sought out God's prophets and killed them. Because of this Elijah was discouraged and afraid. He couldn't take the pressure any more, so he ran far away and hid in a cave on a mountainside.

The Bible says it was there that God found him. In the midst of Elijah's fear and discouragement, when all he wanted to do was run away and hide, God came to him and quietly asked, "What are you doing here, Elijah?"

Elijah gave God an earful. Of how he'd been godly. How he'd been the one to stand for everything God wanted people to do. And now all that didn't seem to matter—to God or anybody. Now he was the only prophet left, and folks were trying to kill him.

So God told Elijah to tuck himself into a crevice in the rocks. And the Bible says a great whirlwind passed by the crevice and tore the rocks apart. A great earthquake then shook the whole mountain. Following the earthquake, a fireball blazed past Elijah. The Bible says Elijah didn't see or hear God in these huge, miraculous upheavals. But then Elijah heard a quiet whisper. It was God asking again, "What are you doing here, Elijah?"

It was then that God told Elijah to leave the mountain. He named three men who would come to Elijah's aid to help destroy the idol worshipers in Israel. God also told Elijah there were seven thousand other godly prophets still left in Israel. Elijah wasn't alone. He wasn't the last guy standing. God had people and resources already prepared that Elijah never even knew about.

Indeed, God always has things under control. He is stronger than a whirlwind, more powerful than an earthquake, greater than any fireball, and much bigger than your joblessness. Yet He is gentle enough to know how much discouragement hurts your heart. In the midst of your hiding and hurting His quiet voice whispers, "I love you. I understand your pain. I have good things in my plan for you that you can't even imagine. It will be all right. Trust Me."

Getting Through Your Day

I had said in my alarm, "I am cut off from your sight." But you heard the voice of my pleas for mercy when I cried to you for help. PSALM 31:22 ESV

You are my hiding place; you protect me from trouble. You surround me with songs of victory. PSALM 32:7 NLT

May Jesus himself and God our Father, who reached out in love and surprised you with gifts of unending help and confidence, put a fresh heart in you, invigorate your work, enliven your speech. 2 THESSALONIANS 2:16–17 MSG

Let your mercy comfort me as you promised. Let your compassion reach me so that I may live, because your teachings make me happy. PSALM 119:76–77 GOD'S WORD

This poor man cried, and the LORD heard him and saved him out of all his troubles. The angel of the LORD encamps around those who fear Him, and rescues them. PSALM 34:6–7 NASB

Such confidence as this is ours through Christ before God. Not that we are competent in ourselves to claim anything for ourselves, but our competence comes from God. 2 CORINTHIANS 3:4–5 NIV

Today I Will...

✓ Remember the example of Elijah when I'm facing overwhelming discouragement. God is stronger than a whirlwind, more powerful than an earthquake, greater than any fireball, and He has everything under control.

✓ Find a place and time to get away and get alone with God. I will pour out my heart to Him and ask Him to touch my life like He never has before, for the Bible says God is a refuge for the oppressed.

✓ Ask God to show me what He might want me to do during this period of unscheduled time in my life. I will try to be open to new opportunities and new ways for work and for helping others.

✓ Be careful to avoid the pleasures of the world. The world encourages me to postpone the inevitable, to satisfy my hurt with pleasures that only last for a moment. I will choose instead to focus my mind and heart on God.

✓ Seek the company of other Christians. Though I need quiet time to sort out life and its difficulties, I also need the fellowship of other Christians who will listen, pray, care, and share insights together with me.

WORDS

Burnt Bridges

Never make light of the king, even in your thoughts. And don't make fun of the powerful, even in your own bedroom. For a little bird might deliver your message and tell them what you said.
ECCLESIASTES 10:20 NLT

When my friend Gordon's last job was terminated, he was shocked. Totally unexpected. Yet when his boss gave him the news that he was no longer needed, Gordon didn't respond with angry words or accusations. He didn't shout about how unfair the decision was. He didn't give vent to his emotions or suggest others, in his opinion, who were more qualified to be downsized. Instead Gordon calmly asked some questions. He wanted to make sure he hadn't done anything wrong and that his boss would give him a recommendation when he applied for another job.

A human resources employee was sitting in the boss's office during this conversation. As Gordon left the room, the human resources person told him he had never seen anyone take the news that he had just been laid off with such level-headedness. Gordon smiled. His mind was reeling. His heart was broken. His dreams were shattered. He felt the decision was unfair. But, because he was familiar with the Bible and because he wanted to honor God, Gordon had been careful with his words. He knew his words would leave an impression. And he knew from past experience that parting shots never help; they only burn the bridge behind you.

Gordon was also well aware of King Solomon's caution found in Ecclesiastes 10:20—the verse that begins this short story. King Solomon knew how quickly bad words can travel. He said that even your bedroom isn't a safe place to curse the rich or revile the king because a little birdie might be listening.

Despite technology, scientific advances, and our modern way of doing things, Solomon's caution is as relevant today as it was centuries ago when it was written. In fact, we could update Solomon's words today to read, "Don't say or do anything you don't want reported on the front page of the newspaper." Whether a stray comment, a furtive e-mail, a whispered phone call, a personal posting on a Web site or blog—you never know if or when whatever you say or write will become public and come back to bite you. It's best to "keep your tongue from evil" (Psalm 34:13 NIV).

Now, as Gordon begins his latest job search, he has asked God for continued help with his words. He has been careful to position his previous employer in a good light. He has tried to follow Solomon's advice whenever anyone asks him about his job loss. Because God has helped him control his words and stay away from the negative, Gordon hasn't burned the bridges of communication, friendship, and respect that had been built at his previous place of employment. As a matter of fact, his boss's boss from this previous job recently gave him a glowing recommendation that has opened all sorts of job opportunities for him.

Solomon would urge you to live your life accordingly. Be careful of what you say, how you say it, and to whom you say it. A job loss can injure your pride, but parting shots can damage you even more. Ask God to place His hand over your mouth if you're tempted to vent something you'd rather not see on the front page of the newspaper. Learn from Solomon to let your words be few. Remember, burnt bridges never help anyone get anywhere.

Getting Through Your Day

Set a guard, O Lord, over my mouth; keep watch over the door of my lips!   PSALM 141:3 ESV

Avoid irreverent, empty speech, for this will produce an even greater measure of godlessness.   2 TIMOTHY 2:16 HCSB

Out of the overflow of the heart the mouth speaks.
                                                MATTHEW 12:34 NIV

Do everything without complaining or arguing, so that you may be innocent and pure as God's perfect children, who live in a world of corrupt and sinful people.   PHILIPPIANS 2:14–15 GNT

Do not let any unwholesome talk come out of your mouths, but only what is helpful for building others up according to their needs, that it may benefit those who listen.   EPHESIANS 4:29 NIV

Be gracious in your speech. The goal is to bring out the best in others in a conversation, not put them down, not cut them out.
                                                COLOSSIANS 4:6 MSG

Don't be in a hurry to talk. Don't be eager to speak in the presence of God. Since God is in heaven and you are on earth, limit the number of your words.   ECCLESIASTES 5:2 GOD'S WORD

Today I Will Get This Off My Chest...

Use the space below to respond to as few or as many of these questions as you like.

• Do you ever act out of frustration and then have to live with your angry words and decisions? What is the Lord revealing to you about this right now?

- What do you do when you get uptight about a situation? How do you respond? What do you have to change in your words and actions so that God will be glorified?
- Have you ever burned a bridge at a former place of employment? Is there something you need to do to make this situation right?
- In Exodus 10:28 Pharaoh told Moses to leave his presence and never return. Pharaoh's ultimatum sounded final, but God had other plans. Ultimately, in Exodus 12:31, Pharaoh summons Moses to his palace because he needs Moses' help. Sound familiar? How have God's plans affected your ultimatums, your final words to someone?

GOD'S SOVEREIGNTY

The Nosedive

*It was not you who sent me here, but God; and He has made
me a father to Pharaoh, and lord of all his house, and a ruler
throughout all the land of Egypt.*   GENESIS 45:8 NKJV

I had to leave in the next five minutes or I'd be late for an
appointment, but the lady on the telephone just wouldn't quit
talking. I tried all of the polite conversational signals to end
our chat, but still she rattled on. Fifteen minutes later she
finally said goodbye. I flew out the door, climbed into the car,
and roared off down the street. But as I drove I noticed flashing
lights in front of me. A horrible car wreck had occurred at the
corner traffic light. I realized the extra minutes spent in that
conversation had kept me indoors, off the street, and safe from
that pileup of twisted metal. I breathed a prayer of thanks for
God's not-so-subtle intrusion into *my* plans, *my* schedule.

While there's nothing wrong with planning out my day
and setting up my schedule, the Bible is very clear that as a
child of God, I am not the one in control of my life. God is.
God alone is the sovereign, supreme ruler over everything. He
is the one who chooses who will rule and who won't. God has
determined in advance what nations should inhabit the whole
earth. He has planned how long they will exist, how many
people will fill them, and "the exact places where they should
live" (Acts 17:26 NIV).

God is intimately involved in the smaller details of life,
too. He knows where His children are at every moment and
has a life plan for each one. The Bible adds that my plans and

schedules can easily be altered if they are not a part of God's life plan for me.

Just ask Joseph. As one of the youngest of twelve brothers, Joseph's life was moving along smoothly. He was his father's right-hand man on the family "sheep ranch." Joseph had had some dreams, too—dreams that included success and status. Life looked good.

But the plans seemed to take a nosedive when his brothers turned on him and sold him to a slave caravan. His first job as a slave fell apart too, and Joseph was thrown into prison. When folks who promised to say a good word about Joseph forgot him for three years, Joseph probably wondered what in the world was going on. What had happened to those big plans, those dreams—his life?

God had happened. God had something in store for Joseph. Eventually God's plan took this son of a sheep rancher, brought him to the attention of the king of Egypt, and promoted him to become the *king's* right-hand man. Joseph's wildest imagination probably never would have dreamed up that plan or that schedule. But this royal ending to his life was part of God's plan for Joseph. And all of it happened because God is sovereign. God is in control.

You have plans, schedules, and dreams too. But God has plans for you, just like He did for Joseph. And God's plans may include some things that will reach far beyond your imaginings. Yet you can be assured that nothing will come into your life that God doesn't know about, that God doesn't ultimately control. If right now your plans seem to have taken a nosedive and your dreams have taken a beating, trust God. The Bible assures you God has a plan for your life, and it's a good one. Remember Joseph.

Getting Through Your Day

I know that you can do all things; no plan of yours can be thwarted.
JOB 42:2 NIV

God does what he wants with the powers of heaven and the people on earth. No one can stop his powerful hand or question what he does.
DANIEL 4:35 NCV

Truly I have spoken; truly I will bring it to pass. I have planned it, surely I will do it.
ISAIAH 46:11 NASB

God and God only has the power to help or hurt your cause.
2 CHRONICLES 25:8 MSG

The LORD does whatever He pleases in heaven and on earth, in the seas and all the depths.
PSALM 135:6 HCSB

Are not two sparrows sold for a penny? Yet not one of them will fall to the ground apart from the will of your Father. And even the very hairs of your head are all numbered. So don't be afraid; you are worth more than many sparrows.
MATTHEW 10:29–31 NIV

Today I Will...

✓ Be thankful that my life is not governed by chance or the twist of fate, but that as a child of God, my life is under His control.
✓ Be grateful for the plan God has for my life, knowing that His plan is a good one, a plan that will give me a future and a hope.

✓ Appreciate the blessings found within this day, even if they are different from what I had hoped for in this time and season of my life.

✓ Be pleased to remember that those things I see as disruptions to my plan and schedule may indeed be God's way of bringing something even better into my life.

✓ Be glad about the unseen ways God is in control of the things of my life. I may not understand it all, but I will praise Him, for He is worthy to be praised.

✓ Value the reminder of the life of Joseph—his dreams and ultimate reality as planned out and brought about by God.

FAITH

Holding My Hand

If I rise on the wings of the dawn, if I settle on the far side of the sea, even there your hand will guide me, your right hand will hold me fast. PSALM 139:9–10 NIV

You can't read much of the Bible without encountering the word *faith*. In fact, you'll find the Bible talks about what some folks call saving faith, living faith, and dying faith.

Saving faith is a gift from God that involves a heart change. The Bible says whenever people acknowledge their sin, turn away from it, and accept Jesus' death on the cross as God's only acceptable payment for that sin, that person is granted God's gift of saving faith. Such faith produces a changed heart that loves God, a changed life that longs to do what He wants, and a changed final destination from Satan's home to God's home.

That's where what's called *dying faith* comes in. The Bible assures you, if you have received salvation by faith, when you die you will be welcomed into heaven. God has "identified you as his own by giving you the Holy Spirit, whom he promised long ago. The Spirit is God's guarantee that he will give [you] the inheritance he promised" (Ephesians 1:13–14 NLT). Part of that promised inheritance is a home in heaven; a guarantee of no more tears, pain, or sorrow; and the expectation of a great celebration at a heavenly supper. Pass the mac and cheese, please!

Between saving faith and dying faith, you'll find what some call *living faith*. Living faith encompasses the day-in, day-out obedient walk of a child of God. It involves going where God says to go, doing what God says to do, living your life in a way that honors Him. When everything is easy and your ride of life is smooth and predictable, functioning by living faith seems easy too. When the road gets rough and the twists and turns become unpredictable, however, faith gets harder.

But why should it? Why should life's trouble spots like a tough economy, joblessness, or the possibility of foreclosure affect your faith? Is God any less God today than He was when you were gainfully employed? Has God's power or strength been diminished because you no longer have a steady income? No. Your head knows that God is still the same mighty, supreme ruler of the cosmos who loves you with an everlasting love. Your circumstances, however, are so frightening and loom so large they can distract you from that marvelous reality.

A story is told of a little boy who had to cross the Alps during a dark winter night in the middle of World War II. He and his father were Jews, and they were fleeing the Nazis. The mountain trail they followed was little more than a goat track that wound precipitously close to the edge of several cliffs. When the little boy safely arrived at an inn on the other side of the mountains, the innkeeper asked him if he had been scared while journeying on such a dangerous path. The young boy thought for a moment and replied, "I was in no danger, sir. I had no need to fear, for my father held my hand."

What a marvelous picture of faith. Follow the example of the little boy and place your fears, circumstances, heartaches, worries—your life—in God's hands. Be assured that He will hold onto you. Focus on that marvelous reality. For that is living faith.

Getting Through Your Day

Faith comes from hearing the Good News, and people hear the Good News when someone tells them about Christ.
ROMANS 10:17 NCV

For we walk by faith, not by sight. 2 CORINTHIANS 5:7 NASB

It is by grace you have been saved, through faith—and this not from yourselves, it is the gift of God—not by works, so that no one can boast. EPHESIANS 2:8–9 NIV

Although you have never seen Christ, you love him. You don't see him now, but you believe in him. You are extremely happy with joy and praise that can hardly be expressed in words as you obtain the salvation that is the goal of your faith.
1 PETER 1:8–9 GOD'S WORD

It's impossible to please God apart from faith. And why? Because anyone who wants to approach God must believe both that he exists and that he cares enough to respond to those who seek him. HEBREWS 11:6 MSG

Truly, I say to you, if you have faith like a grain of mustard seed, you will say to this mountain, "Move from here to there," and it will move, and nothing will be impossible for you.
MATTHEW 17:20 ESV

Today I Will Remember...

Life has dimensions other than those that can be encompassed by the senses, and into those dimensions nothing can enter except the principle of faith. G. CAMPBELL MORGAN

Believe God's love and power more than you believe your own feelings and experiences. Your Rock is Christ, and it is not the *rock* that ebbs and flows, but the sea.

SAMUEL RUTHERFORD

Christ never failed to distinguish between doubt and unbelief. Doubt is *can't believe*. Unbelief is *won't believe*. Doubt is honesty. Unbelief is obstinacy. Doubt is looking for light. Unbelief is content with darkness. HENRY DRUMMOND

Never try to arouse faith from within. You cannot stir up faith from the depths of your heart. Leave your heart, and look into the face of Christ. ANDREW MURRAY

Faith is deliberate confidence in the character of God whose ways you may not understand at the time.

OSWALD CHAMBERS

PERSONALIZE THE RIDE

Use these honest questions to help you think through what you've read about anger, discouragement, your words, God's sovereignty, and faith. Record your thoughts in response to as many or as few of these questions as you like so you will have a good reminder of your journey later on.

- Are you having trouble with anger or discouragement? What is causing you the most pain?
- What do you want God to know today? (Be honest with your words; God is all knowing.)
- Has God's power or strength been diminished because you no longer have a steady income? What can you do or say or write to remind yourself of God's powerful dealings in your life?
- How is living faith helping you get through today? How has your saving faith made a difference to your roller-coaster ride of unemployment?
- I am thankful today for… (There is always something to thank God for!)

4

THE TUNNEL

The best roller-coaster rides don't happen by accident. Each segment of a great thrill ride is carefully crafted so that riders rarely see the next portion of the ride. One of the most unexpected parts of a roller-coaster ride is the descent into the tunnel. Roller-coaster builders know if riders are surprised by entering a tunnel, the thrill of the entire ride is enhanced. These same engineers also know just how long the tunnel should be. Too long, and riders will become bored. Too short, and the whole tunnel experience won't have a chance to register on the brain. If the engineers can orchestrate a twist or bend in the middle of the tunnel, all the better. Riders won't be able to catch their breath until they catch a glimpse of daylight at the tunnel's end.

Your unemployment roller-coaster ride has its own tunnel experience too. After twirling in the loop-the-loop of up-and-down emotions, you can easily find yourself dropped into the darkness of the unexpected once again. In fact, when you lost your job you probably thought the job offers would come quickly, the leads would come without a problem. Remember how those friends or work acquaintances said you were such a good employee? How they said they'd hire you in a minute because you were so valuable? Now that you're unemployed, these same folks won't even return your phone calls. Their hollow compliments leave you stumbling in the dark. There seem to be few options and no light at the end of this tunnel.

Nonetheless, if you were to stop in the middle of a roller-coaster tunnel, you might be surprised by what you'd find. Roller-coaster builders usually install a small walkway along the inside of the tunnel. Nothing fancy. It's more for the maintenance guys so they can check the tracks before the ride begins every day. You'd also find some lights in the tunnel. Not big ones, though. They're usually covered, so they give off very little light during the ride. But the lights are there nonetheless. You would also notice that the tracks inside the tunnel are exactly like the tracks on the rest of the ride.

So what does this mean to you and your unemployment ride? While your descent into the unemployment tunnel seems to leave you searching in the dark, there is a walkway through this tunnel—the walkway of God's guidance. The lights in your unemployment tunnel are there as well. They may not be shining brightly right now, but you can choose to let the lights of family and friends, hope, gratitude, and generosity shine more brightly for you during this tunnel time. And the tracks? The ones that are exactly the same inside and outside the tunnel? That sameness is a reminder that the God you have met thus far in your unemployment ride is still the same loving God who cares about you. He knows right where you are in the middle of that dark tunnel. And He has given you a lamp—the Bible—to shine for you in this dark time (Psalm 119:105). Let God's light illumine you now as you look more closely at guidance, worry, family and friends, gratitude, courage, and generosity.

GUIDANCE

Why Do You Want God's Guidance?

*I know, God, that mere mortals can't run
their own lives, that men and women don't have what
it takes to take charge of life.* JEREMIAH 10:23 MSG

There are days in the unemployment ride when I feel like one of the two vultures in the Disney animated version of *Robin Hood*. The two vultures are standing guard when one of them asks the other, "What are we gonna do now?" The second vulture shrugs its feathery shoulders and replies, "I dunno. What do you want to do?" The first vulture shrugs back in reply and answers, "I dunno. What do *you* want to do?" That wishy-washy, undecided, unsure-of-what-to-do-next predicament often marks my jobless days. It sure would be nice if I could get a little guidance.

But even as I thought about asking God for guidance, I was struck with a strange question. *Why did I want God's guidance?* I'd been busy asking *what* to do next, but not once since my layoff had I clarified *why* I wanted God's action on my behalf. There were plenty of resources available to help me write resumes, build job networks, and determine suitable career directions based on my personality type, but none of these practical guides addressed the "why" of my guidance dilemma. *So why did I want God's guidance in my job search in the first place?*

My mind whirled. I realized I had been a bit manipulative in my guidance prayers thus far. I had said I wanted God to guide me, but I had been holding onto a hidden agenda. I was seeking guidance, sure, but also determining how that guidance should pan out. My prayers had treated God like a genie in a bottle. I had been playing a mental mind game with Him, praying for guidance when really what I wanted was His direction to a perfect, secure job so I'd never have to go through unemployment again. Now the question "Why do you want God to guide you?" had blown that hidden agenda apart.

As I sorted through my attitudes and actions, I realized that asking God to guide me meant something greater than merely asking Him to implement my ideas. Asking God for guidance meant I would have to relinquish my will for His. Asking God for guidance meant giving up my dreams for work, career, success, and life and accepting His dreams for me instead. Asking God for guidance meant trusting God to work out *His* best plan for my life. Asking God for guidance meant placing my life, my joblessness, and my future in His hands—with no hidden agendas, no limitations on what God could do.

So why did I want God to guide me? As I thought it through, the reason became clear. I wanted God's guidance because I love Him and I know that He loves me. I want to want what He wants. The Bible says I can trust God to direct my path, to work on my behalf, and to bring me where He wants me to be when I need to be there.

When I finished this thought process, there was such a feeling of relief! With the "why" settled, I finally felt ready to work on the "what" of God's guidance, knowing that whatever God has for me will be okay. I just need to trust Him.

So here's a question for you: why do *you* want God's guidance?

Getting Through Your Day

Trust in the LORD with all your heart and lean not on your own understanding; in all your ways acknowledge him, and he will make your paths straight.   PROVERBS 3:5–6 NIV

You, LORD, are my light; you dispel my darkness.
                                               2 SAMUEL 22:29 GNT

The LORD will always lead you, satisfy you in a parched land, and strengthen your bones. You will be like a watered garden and like a spring whose waters never run dry.   ISAIAH 58:11 HCSB

Commit your works to the LORD, and your thoughts will be established.   PROVERBS 16:3 NKJV

Tell the next generation that this is God, our God forever and ever. He will guide us forever.   PSALM 48:13–14 ESV

I will instruct you and show you the way to go; with My eye on you, I will give counsel.   PSALM 32:8 HCSB

Today I Will...

✓ Remember to be teachable, like Paul. Though Paul wanted to go in one direction, God guided him another way. Because Paul remained teachable he easily recognized when God closed one door and opened another.

✓ Jog my memory when I find it hard to sense God's guidance. I will recall the point where I last felt sure of His direction. I will ask Him to show me anything I have forgotten to do or failed to obey, knowing that by removing obstructions His guidance often becomes clearer.

✓ Refuse to second-guess God. I am to walk by faith, but God has also told me to stand firm. Those seemingly contradictory commands merely mean I need to stay so close to God in prayer, praise, and study of His Word that I'll always hear His voice and never have to second-guess Him.

✓ Understand God's guidance isn't mysterious. If the traffic light is red or yellow, I am wise to wait for the green light. So it is with God's guidance. When situations concur with the inward prompting of God's Holy Spirit, then I'll move forward with that green light. When there is a shadow of doubt, I'll wait.

✓ Check out every decision I make with God first. When trusted advisors say a way is right, they might be wrong. Nathan told David to build the temple, but God said no. Joab told Adonijah to become king, but God said no. I will seek God's mind on every decision so that I will keep walking in God's way.

WORRY

At Wit's End

*Do not worry about tomorrow; it will have enough worries
of its own. There is no need to add to the troubles
each day brings.* MATTHEW 6:34 GNT

It was midnight. Charlie was still wide awake, replaying the day's events in his mind. For weeks he had sensed something was up at work. Today he had learned just what that something was. He had walked into the conference room and had seen his boss sitting next to the man from human resources. The boss's words had been a blur. Tough times... Had to make cuts... We appreciate all you've done... We'll take your keys and pass card... Leave the building by 10:00 a.m. The meeting had been over that quickly. Charlie had packed up and gotten out by 9:45 a.m., but he'd gone through the motions as if he'd been in a dream. A bad dream that didn't end.

Charlie had gone home and told his family about the job loss. The kids were the last to hear the news that evening at the supper table. But now it was midnight. Everyone else was asleep, yet Charlie couldn't unwind. His mind kept churning. He realized what little severance pay he received would last only a few weeks. His medical coverage would drop off soon, too. The knot in his stomach grew as he tried to figure out how he would be able to pay the bills and keep the house. An hour later Charlie was so stirred up with worry, he felt like he was losing his mind. That was when Charlie began to pray.

The Bible is full of reminders to turn away from worry, but when the harsh reality of a situation hits, those reminders are sometimes easier to say than do. You can find yourself in the same place as Charlie—desperate, scared, and almost frantic with worry.

Psalm 107 tells of some merchants who went to sea on large ships. They were experienced, capable sailors who knew when to outrun a storm and when to put into a port and wait things out. Yet these capable men found themselves inexplicably caught in the middle of a terrible tempest. The wind blew the waves taller than they had ever seen. Their troughs went deeper than the sailors could have imagined. The psalmist says "in their peril their courage melted away" (Psalm 107:26 NIV).

Just like Charlie, the sailors of Psalm 107 were at their wit's end. And, just like Charlie, the sailors finally cried out to God. In that moment God heard the cries of the worried men and brought them out of their trouble. God stilled the storm, calmed the waves, and guided the sailors to a safe harbor. The psalmist doesn't say how long this took. He doesn't give details of how God did everything. He merely assures readers that God heard the sailors' prayer and understood their need. God provided all that was necessary to deliver them from their distress and worry. All the sailors had to do was pray and trust God to help them.

It looks like Charlie had the right idea that night. By bringing his worries to God, he was able to focus on God's greatness instead of his own desperate circumstances. With a renewed trust in God, Charlie could think more clearly and assess the situation. Now Charlie prays immediately when worries threaten. He knows that because of God's constancy and faithfulness to fulfill His promises, worry isn't worth the effort. Trusting God is.

Getting Through Your Day

Do not worry, saying, "What shall we eat?" or "What shall we drink?" or "What shall we wear?" For the pagans run after all these things, and your heavenly Father knows that you need them. But seek first his kingdom and his righteousness, and all these things will be given to you as well.   MATTHEW 6:31–33 NIV

Blessed is the man who trusts in the LORD, whose trust is the LORD. He is like a tree planted by water, that sends out its roots by the stream, and does not fear when heat comes, for its leaves remain green, and is not anxious in the year of drought, for it does not cease to bear fruit.   JEREMIAH 17:7–8 ESV

In the fear of the LORD there is strong confidence, and his children will have a place of refuge.   PROVERBS 14:26 GOD'S WORD

Jesus said to his followers, "So I tell you, don't worry about the food you need to live, or about the clothes you need for your body. Life is more than food, and the body is more than clothes. Look at the birds. They don't plant or harvest, they don't have storerooms or barns, but God feeds them. And you are worth much more than birds. You cannot add any time to your life by worrying about it. If you cannot do even the little things, then why worry about the big things?"   LUKE 12:22–26 NCV

Today I Will Remember...

Worry is a thin stream of fear trickling through the mind. If encouraged, it cuts a channel into which all other thoughts are drained.   ARTHUR SOMERS ROCHE

Worry is the interest we pay on tomorrow's trouble.

E. STANLEY JONES

Worry, like a rocking chair, will give you something to do, but it won't get you anywhere. VANCE HAVNER

What does your anxiety do? It does not empty tomorrow of its sorrow, but it empties today of its strength. It does not make you escape the evil—it makes you unfit to cope with it if it comes. IAN MACLAREN

Worry affects the circulation, the heart, the glands, the whole nervous system, and profoundly affects the health. I have never known a man who died from overwork, but many who died from doubt. CHARLES W. MAYO

FAMILY AND FRIENDS

The Elephant in the Room

Though one may be overpowered, two can defend themselves. A cord of three strands is not quickly broken. ECCLESIASTES 4:12 NIV

I have a close friend who is gainfully employed as a book-keeper. We'll occasionally go out to lunch—her treat, since I'm not working. She'll inquire about my job searches, my family, and life in general, and I'll tell her about the challenges of buying groceries with higher prices and no income. As we ate lunch one day she assured me she had been praying about my circumstances. She added that she really felt terrible about my unemployment situation but was also glad that these problems were happening to me and not to her!

I burst out laughing. This friend had said aloud what so many people around me seem to be thinking. Friends feel awkward when I'm around because they still have their jobs and I don't. Folks don't know what to say because they can't make my situation any better. Some are even afraid to be around me, fearful that my unemployment will rub off on them. Family members feel some of these things too and share my concern over my job loss because it directly affects their purchasing power. All of these feelings make up what psychologists call "survivor guilt." And it's my guess that your friends and family might have some of these feelings too.

When you're unemployed there are many things in your life you can no longer control. But there's good news. You *can* control the impact of survivor guilt on your friends and family. Just because you don't have a job or a regular paycheck every week, your friends and family don't have to feel guilty if they *do* have work, money, or the things you no longer have. God can bless them, and you can rejoice with them in that blessing. When you do that, you are giving your friends and family the permission they need to live the life God has given them without having to feel guilty that you don't have what they have.

Your friends and family also need you to bring up discussions about the unemployment problem everyone knows about but won't talk about, that proverbial "elephant in the room." They want to help, but they don't want to offend. You might offer some practical ways for them to help you through this time. By bringing up the subject of your unemployment, you can help everyone breathe a sigh of relief.

Not only do your friends and family need your help through this transition time, you also need them and their support during this unemployment ride. Their prayers, encouraging words, and willingness to come alongside and bear your burdens can help lift the weight of your joblessness from your shoulders for a little while.

If your friends and family don't feel comfortable around you while you're unemployed, they'll find themselves standing alone, merely looking on while you ride the roller coaster of unemployment. And, if you cut yourself off from friends and family during your joblessness, you will be standing alone. The Bible says that's no way to live. You need your friends and family right now as much as they need you. If you stand together during your joblessness, you'll be able to defend one another against the enemies of discouragement, guilt, and fear and also laugh together at the joys that will come your way.

Getting Through Your Day

Be careful! Watch out and don't forget the things you have seen. Don't forget them as long as you live, but teach them to your children and grandchildren.   DEUTERONOMY 4:9 NCV

If someone says, "I love God," and hates his brother, he is a liar; for the one who does not love his brother whom he has seen, cannot love God whom he has not seen. And this commandment we have from Him, that the one who loves God should love his brother also.   1 JOHN 4:20–21 NASB

Friends love through all kinds of weather, and families stick together in all kinds of trouble.   PROVERBS 17:17 MSG

Oil and incense bring joy to the heart, and the sweetness of a friend is better than self-counsel.   PROVERBS 27:9 HCSB

Two people are better than one, because they get more done by working together. If one falls down, the other can help him up. But it is bad for the person who is alone and falls, because no one is there to help.   ECCLESIASTES 4:9–10 NCV

If anyone does not provide for his relatives, and especially for his immediate family, he has denied the faith and is worse than an unbeliever.   1 TIMOTHY 5:8 NIV

Today I Will Pray...

✓ For my friends and thank God for their care and concern. I will ask God to continue to bless them and to give me a heart that easily rejoices in those blessings.

✓ That God will strengthen my family and give them peace during my time of joblessness. I will give thanks to God for them and remember they mean well, even if their ways aggravate me sometimes.

✓ For a greater understanding between me and my friends and family, so that we will be stronger and more closely knit once we are on the other side of this career transition time.

✓ For a time of joy and refreshment for my friends, family, and myself. Such joy only comes from God, but to share such joy with my loved ones would be an added blessing.

✓ And ask God to show me a creative way to show my gratefulness to my friends and family, to celebrate their love for me, and to let them know how much I value each one.

✓ For a change in my spirit to be more loyal and giving to my family and friends. Jesus was this type of friend to His disciples, so I'll ask God to change my heart to be more like His.

GRATITUDE

With a Grateful Heart

*Enter into His gates with thanksgiving, and
into His courts with praise. Be thankful to Him,
and bless His name.*   PSALM 100:4 NKJV

Depending on traffic, stoplights, and other delays, it can take me from ten to twenty minutes to get to church. Not too long ago I was making this trek from my home with fewer hours of sleep than I should have had. I was trying to shake the cobwebs from my brain as I drove, but the usual waker-uppers—windows open so that cold breezes could blow in my face, radio blasting a favorite tune as loud as my car speakers could bear, periodic pinches on my arms and legs—just weren't doing the trick. I knew I had to engage more than my senses alone to become fully wakeful, so I started to play a little mind game, something I hoped would help overcome my sleepiness.

I remembered King David had penned Psalm 100, urging God's children to come into "His gates with thanksgiving." I wondered what would happen if I tried to think of things to be thankful for. Maybe that would help wake me up. I started with the obvious things around me and said aloud, "Lord, I thank you for... puppy dogs. Tiny kittens. Blue skies. Puffy white clouds. That soaring hawk. The flash of that bluebird's wing. The smell of wood smoke. The aroma of freshly baked bread. The scent of hyacinths heralding spring. A whiff of garlic outside that pizza place. The taste of my favorite food. The feel of soft fur." All were things my senses could acknowledge. Each one was something I was thankful for.

I kept up my mind game and my audible prayer of gratitude, thanking the Lord for my immediate family. I named each one by name and highlighted one specific thing about each one that usually made me smile. Then I broadened my family circle to include the cousins, aunts, uncles, nieces, nephews, in-laws (and out-laws!). By this point I was well down the road. The radio had long since stopped blaring its music. The windows had been closed for several miles. But I was waking up, and my mind was engaged in the exercise too.

So I kept on thanking the Lord, expressing grateful thoughts about God's children, my family in Him. For those in my local church, for those who had been kind to me during this recent job loss, for those I'd been privileged to know over the years. Again I named each one by name and remembered a kindness or character trait that made my heart smile when I acknowledged them.

All the way to church that day I kept up my thanksgiving, widening my circle of appreciation to include my home, my community, my country, and all those who had suffered or given their lives to make my freedoms possible. By the time I pulled into the church parking lot I was wide awake—and weeping. Not weeping from sadness, though. This cry came from deep within, it's true, but this was a cry of gratefulness.

I still didn't have two nickels to rub together. I still didn't have a job to go to the next day. I still didn't have any clue how long I would be unemployed. But I did have one thing—a grateful heart. God had given me so many blessings, so many good things, I just had to say thanks.

Getting Through Your Day

*"Give thanks to the L*ORD*, because he is good; his love is eternal!" Repeat these words in praise to the L*ORD*, all you whom he has saved.*   PSALM 107:1–2 GNT

Let the message about the Messiah dwell richly among you, teaching and admonishing one another in all wisdom, and singing psalms, hymns, and spiritual songs, with gratitude in your hearts to God. And whatever you do, in word or in deed, do everything in the name of the Lord Jesus, giving thanks to God the Father through Him.   COLOSSIANS 3:16–17 HCSB

*Give thanks to the L*ORD*, for he is good. His love endures forever. Give thanks to the God of gods. His love endures forever. Give thanks to the Lord of lords: His love endures forever.*   PSALM 136:1–3 NIV

In everything give thanks; for this is the will of God in Christ Jesus for you.   1 THESSALONIANS 5:18 NKJV

Thank God! Call out his Name! Tell the whole world who he is and what he's done!   1 CHRONICLES 16:8 MSG

Therefore, we must be thankful that we have a kingdom that cannot be shaken. Because we are thankful, we must serve God with fear and awe in a way that pleases him.   HEBREWS 12:28 GOD'S WORD

Today I Will...

✓ Be thankful that God loves me and has given me the gift of eternal life through Jesus Christ His Son.

✓ Be grateful for the blessings from God that I can see, hear, taste, and touch.

✓ Appreciate my family with all their quirks and failings, for they are God's gift to me.

✓ Be pleased to remember that this day is the day the Lord has given me. He wants me to rejoice and be glad in it.

✓ Be glad that God has blessed me with the opportunity to live in a free country where I can worship, pray, and read the Bible without fear.

✓ Value my Christian brothers and sisters who stand with me as part of God's family—to care for, pray for, and grow together in faith with each other.

COURAGE

The Lifeline

Because the hand of the LORD my God was on me,
I took courage. EZRA 7:28 NIV

Ezra was an Old Testament scribe. A scribe spent every working day hand-copying God's law from old scrolls onto new scrolls. There was no room for error, for this was God's law. The copy had to be an exact duplicate. Because this was Ezra's job, he grew familiar with the law of the Lord. In fact, he loved to study it and tried to obey all the things God said to do.

When Ezra was given the opportunity to move away from Babylon, where he had grown up, back to the Israelite's homeland in Canaan, Ezra jumped at the chance. He wanted to move back to Canaan so that he could continue to study God's law and teach it to others, too.

The king of Babylon knew Ezra. When Ezra announced his intention to return to Canaan, the king asked him to be his official envoy to restock God's temple in Jerusalem. Ezra agreed.

The trip from Babylon to Jerusalem was a long and dangerous one. Travelers would journey together for safety from sandstorms, perilous cliff-side trails, and robber-infested passes between the mountains. The Bible says it took Ezra four months to go the distance but that he made the trip without difficulty because "the gracious hand of his God was on him" (Ezra 7:9 HCSB). The Bible also says it was Ezra's knowledge of God's hand with him that gave him the courage he needed to make the trip and do the job the king had asked him to do.

So why would it matter to Ezra to know for certain that God's hand and presence was with him? Why would that knowledge bring him courage? Ezra knew from studying God's law that God's presence brings His power. When God is with you, God's power and might and strength and authority are all working together on your behalf. Jesus reminded His followers that if God's presence is with you, if His hand is on your life, nothing is impossible for God to do in your life, either.

This promise dangles like a courage lifeline you can cling to, especially when you're unemployed. You face days of discouragement and weariness. You see no way to put the pieces of life back together. But because God's presence is with you, His hand is on your life. You can hear Jesus say to your heart, "Nothing is impossible with God." Amazingly, as you internalize this promise, you find the courage to go on.

So what do you do when the bills are looming, the rent is due, and your income is limited? You remember God is with you; nothing is impossible with God. As you remember, you find the courage to trust Him to provide. What if there are no interviews, no new job leads? God is with you; nothing is impossible for God. No matter what this unemployment roller coaster throws at you, square your shoulders with courage by trusting God, by remembering God's presence is with you. *Nothing* is impossible for God.

As you sense God's abiding presence in your life, you'll find yourself living like Ezra. You'll be able to ride this unemployment roller coaster and complete each task as it comes because, just as it did for Ezra, the "gracious hand of God" will give you the courage to do so.

Getting Through Your Day

Have I not commanded you? Be strong and courageous. Do not be terrified; do not be discouraged, for the LORD your God will be with you wherever you go. JOSHUA 1:9 NIV

Turn your burdens over to the LORD, and he will take care of you. He will never let the righteous person stumble.

PSALM 55:22 GOD'S WORD

For I, the LORD your God, hold your right hand; it is I who say to you, "Fear not, I am the one who helps you." ISAIAH 41:13 ESV

Be strong and courageous, and do the work. Do not be afraid or discouraged, for the LORD God, my God, is with you. He will not fail you or forsake you. 1 CHRONICLES 28:20 NIV

Don't be afraid, little flock, because your Father delights to give you the kingdom. LUKE 12:32 HCSB

Wait for the LORD; be strong and let your heart take courage; yes, wait for the LORD. PSALM 27:14 NASB

Today I Will Pray...

✓ For the courage to believe that God will help me through this journey of joblessness, remembering Ezra's example and the courage he found as he stepped out and moved forward with God.
✓ For a better attitude when things around me seem imperfect or unfair. Such an attitude will help me face my days with courageous optimism, knowing that

God will turn those situations around if and when He wants to.

✓ For the courage needed to face the consequences of my actions, knowing that I have made some mistakes in the past that may cause myself and my loved ones additional pain at this time.

✓ For a new vision, a new dream, a new start, knowing that it takes courage to dream and plan for the future. I'll remember as I pray that fear can paralyze me, but faith will move me forward.

✓ Pray for a quick mind to remember Bible verses that assure me of God's care so that I will find courage and not fear when situations arise that concern me (see "Getting Through Your Day" on the previous page).

✓ Pray for a daring faith that courageously stands firm in a confident trust in God—no matter what happens, no matter what others say, no matter how long it takes.

GENEROSITY

Anything Means Anything

Do not forget to do good to others, and share with them, because
such sacrifices please God. HEBREWS 13:16 NCV

The mail requests. The nonprofit phone calls. The grocery story bell ringer. All wanted the same thing—money. I had always been able to give before, answering every request with a small donation. But here was one more thing unemployment had taken from me—my ability to be generous. I now threw the mailed requests away without opening the envelopes. I ducked my head when walking past the bell ringer to avoid eye contact. I even asked the nonprofit callers to take me off their lists.

Yet even though I knew I didn't have any extra money to give away, closing my wallet to others' needs didn't make me feel very good about myself or very godly, either. I knew the Bible clearly said God's children should be generous in their dealings with others because He has generously given us grace, mercy, forgiveness, and the gift of His Son. I knew all this, but I was stumped and discouraged. How was I supposed to be generous and fulfill what God wanted me to do when I didn't have any money to be generous with, when I didn't have anything extra to give?

Then in Bible study we discussed Barzillai, a little known fellow who had generously provided for King David and his men during David's stay in Mahanaim. In fact Barzillai and his buddies "brought bedding and bowls and articles of pottery. They also brought wheat and barley, flour and roasted grain, beans and lentils, honey and curds, sheep, and cheese from cows' milk for David and his people to eat" (2 Samuel 17:28–29 NIV). Now that was generosity. That was what I used to do, too—what I wanted to do, but couldn't.

But as I stopped and looked more closely at Barzillai's gifts to David, I noticed bedding and pottery. Grain and beans. Milk and cheese. Barzillai's philanthropy wasn't money driven. There wasn't a bag of gold coins in the mix. Instead, Barzillai had given to David and his men the things that were available to Barzillai at the time.

Suddenly, I understood. I had thought because I didn't have lots of money to give away that I didn't have any means to be generous, that I didn't have anything to give to anyone. Yet Barzillai's example showed I could be generous—with anything. While Barzillai had been wealthy enough to provide food and supplies for the king, I remembered the Bible stories of a poor widow who gave God only two tiny coins, a nameless lad who shared a small lunch, and a Samaritan traveler who offered an injured man a bandage, a ride, and a room. My giving didn't have to be limited to dollars and cents. I could also give of my time and talents, my words of encouragement, or prayers of intercession.

As I drove home that day God brought limitless possibilities for generosity to mind. A neighbor was facing hip surgery. He'd need a helper to run errands. A friend was sick with the flu. She could use a dog walker tomorrow. A man from church had just been laid off. I could make a phone call or send an encouraging note. And I could probably scrape together a quarter for the bell ringer, too. Though unemployed, I *could* be generous again. With anything.

Getting Through Your Day

[Jesus] said to them, "Take care, and be on your guard against all covetousness, for one's life does not consist in the abundance of his possessions."   LUKE 12:15 ESV

You are enriched in every way for all generosity, which produces thanksgiving to God through us… Through the proof of this service, they will glorify God for your obedience to the confession of the gospel of Christ, and for your generosity in sharing with them and with others.   2 CORINTHIANS 9:11, 13 HCSB

Don't store up treasures here on earth, where moths eat them and rust destroys them, and where thieves break in and steal. Store your treasures in heaven, where moths and rust cannot destroy, and thieves do not break in and steal. Wherever your treasure is, there the desires of your heart will also be.
            MATTHEW 6:19–21 NLT

We should remember the words that the Lord Jesus said, "Giving gifts is more satisfying than receiving them."
            ACTS 20:35 GOD'S WORD

Freely you received, freely give.   MATTHEW 10:8 NASB

God doesn't miss anything. He knows perfectly well all the love you've shown him by helping needy Christians, and that you keep at it.   HEBREWS 6:10 MSG

Today I Will...

✓ Pray with open hands, not closed fists, and offer all that I am and have to God, asking Him to show me how to be more generous with what I am and have.

✓ Look for ways to be more generous—and not just with my excess.

✓ Think about situations in which I can serve as a host rather than a guest and generously volunteer my time. (Examples might include being a greeter at church, caring for tots in the nursery, administering a food program for the hungry, or hosting a neighborhood watch meeting.)

✓ Explore ways to be more generous in using my spiritual gifts for the benefit of others. I'll act on these ideas, too, rather than wait for someone to come and ask me to help.

✓ Remember to give back to the Lord a portion of everything I receive with a cheerful, willing heart.

✓ Find ways to be generous with the things I can make or do by hand, whether a meal, a painting, a chore for a neighbor, or making a small gift, knowing that when I give to others in this way the Lord is pleased.

✓ Keep in mind that generosity should be a way of life for me since God has been more than generous to me by granting me salvation and an eternal life with Him.

PERSONALIZE THE RIDE

Use this space to clarify and record your thoughts about your ride. It will help relieve pressure and be a good reminder of your thoughts and actions later on. Here are a few honest questions to get you started. Answer as few or as many as you like.

- How have the reminders about worry and family affected you?
- How will God's presence and the courage it brings affect your day?
- What do I want God to know today about my feelings, my worries, my fears?
- Is there an action you can take to be more generous or to find God's guidance?
- I am thankful today for... (There is always something to thank God for!)

5

THE BUNNY HILLS

By the time folks on a roller-coaster ride emerge from the tunnel, they've probably screamed their lungs out. They've probably wrenched a few muscles in their backs, too, because they've braced themselves for whatever might come next in the ride. However, roller-coaster designers know they can't keep the ride going forever. Shortly before the ride ends, they'll include a section of successively smaller ups and downs as a means of slowing the forward momentum of the coaster car.

When roller-coaster riders hit these "bunny hills," they do so unknowingly. They brace themselves for another spin, climb, or dark abyss. But as the foreshortened hill takes an abrupt drop, riders' heads often snap up and down in response to the unexpected downward movement. And just as suddenly, another smaller bunny hill carries them up and immediately back down, repeating the process. If you listen carefully at this point, coaster riders' screams are usually replaced with what sounds like an ooooOOOOoooo, oooOOOooo, ooOOoo— almost an up and down heaving of vocalization. Like a little bit of nausea mixed with a little bit of laughter.

The roller-coaster ride of unemployment will bring you to its own bunny hills. It's bad enough to twist and turn in the loop-the-loop of anger and discouragement when you lose your job. It's tougher still to drop into the tunnel of worry and wonder what to do next. Yet when you hit the bunny hills of joblessness, your emotions and faith can be stretched yet again. By this point in your unemployment ride, you might be on an uphill notion that you'll get something soon, that there's nothing to worry about, but suddenly and unexpectedly you'll get the head-snapping drop of a bunny hill. You might apply for what looks like a sure thing, but for some reason it doesn't pan out. You might be scheduled for an interview that leads nowhere, a request for a resume that never generates a phone call. Maybe a short-term job solution will come, but nothing more, nothing permanent. The successive ups and downs of maybe yes, sorry no, can disturb your emotional and spiritual equilibrium. The unemployment bunny hills can truly mimic that portion of a roller-coaster ride. But there's hope.

Abraham's servant may have had bunny-hill, up-and-down feelings when he went searching for a bride for Isaac. However, the servant successfully navigated those ups and downs by remembering to trust God for every step of his journey. In Genesis 24:42 the servant prayed, "If you will, please grant success to the journey on which I have come" (NIV). Those three words, "if you will," are the keys to surviving the ups and downs of the bunny hills. "If you will" means you're not in charge—God is. "If you will" means things may not happen the way you think would be best—you need to trust God to bring about His will. "If you will" means your plans, schedules, interviews, and job situations are entrusted to God's direction and timing.

As you traverse these bunny hills of unemployment, remember to make "if you will" a part of your prayers. Then take some time to hear what God would say to your heart about hope, timing, endurance, God's provision, and blessings.

HOPE

Someone's Looking for Me

Put your hope in the LORD. For there is faithful love with the LORD, and with Him is redemption in abundance. PSALM 130:7 HCSB

The man was kind, but that didn't stop the sting of yet another rejection. "You have the skills we need," he said, "but we cannot afford to hire someone right now. We've put all our current job openings on hold. I'm sorry." The man's polite appreciation for my skills, however, didn't stop the familiar click as the telephone connection terminated with another negative result.

How many did that make now? Fifteen? Twenty? I had lost count of how many conversations had followed this same track. I felt like I had been kicked in the gut. And what made it worse was that I had really, *really* thought this was *the* job. The job I could sink my teeth into. I had dared to hope a little, and bam! Kicked again. *How long must I wait, God?* I wondered. *How can I even hope for anything when every door is slammed in my face?*

But then I thought about Paul. The apostle Paul might have felt hopeless, too, when he sat alone in Tarsus. As a young man Paul had worked for the Jewish authorities, persecuting every Christian he could find. One day on his way to Damascus, Jesus appeared to Paul in a vision, asking him why he was persecuting Christians. The vision blinded Paul. He stumbled the rest of the way into the city and waited there for a visitor who taught him about Jesus. When Paul came to believe in Jesus as his Savior and Messiah, the Bible says his sight was restored.

Paul was excited. God had touched his heart in a marvelous way. He wanted to share this message with others. Understandably, many Christians were nervous to have him around.

They weren't sure if his conversion was genuine. Because folks couldn't trust him, church leaders sent Paul away, back to his hometown of Tarsus.

The Bible doesn't say what Paul did for the next eighteen months in Tarsus, but you can probably imagine some of it. Because Paul no longer had his "job" persecuting Christians, he had to find work. It might have been during this time that he learned to make tents. Though it was an occupation that would pay his way later on, the life skills that Paul possessed as a Bible teacher and public speaker languished in Tarsus. To spend eighteen months on the shelf—eighteen months without his skills being wanted or needed—could have been a hopeless situation for Paul.

But Paul chose to put his hope in the Lord, and the Lord did not forget him. As the church began to grow and spread beyond Jerusalem's borders, church leaders remembered Paul's skills as a teacher and speaker. So Barnabas was sent to Tarsus to look for Paul.

As I remembered the story of Paul, and Barnabas's journey to find him, I found hope. Not in my skills or abilities. Not in my network or spiffed-up resume. I found hope in the Lord, for that's where my trust must center. Maybe there will be more rejections to my job inquiries, but I'll hold onto hope. God sent someone to look for Paul so he could do the work God had prepared for him. One of these days God will send someone looking for me too. I'm hoping for it.

Getting Through Your Day

Show me the right path, O Lord; point out the road for me to follow. Lead me by your truth and teach me, for you are the God who saves me. All day long I put my hope in you.

PSALM 25:4–5 NLT

Happy are those who are helped by the God of Jacob. Their hope is in the LORD their God. He made heaven and earth, the sea and everything in it. He remains loyal forever. PSALM 146:5–6 NCV

Uphold me according to your promise, that I may live, and let me not be put to shame in my hope! Hold me up, that I may be safe. PSALM 119:116–117 ESV

Why am I so sad? Why am I so troubled? I will put my hope in God, and once again I will praise him, my savior and my God. PSALM 43:5 GNT

The LORD's eyes are on those who fear him, on those who wait with hope for his mercy. PSALM 33:18 GOD'S WORD

Today I Will Remember...

There is not enough darkness in all the world to put out the light of one small candle. ANONYMOUS

The natural flights of the human mind are not from pleasure to pleasure but from hope to hope. SAMUEL JOHNSON

Oh, remember this: There is never a time when we may not hope in God. Whatever our necessities, however great our difficulties, and though to all appearance help is impossible, yet our business is to hope in God, and it will be found that it is not in vain. GEORGE MÜLLER

Everything that is done in the world is done by hope. No merchant or tradesman would set himself to work if he did not hope to reap benefit thereby. MARTIN LUTHER

In the presence of hope, faith is born.

ROBERT HAROLD SCHULLER

Do not look forward to the changes and chances of this life in fear; rather look to them with full hope that, as they arise, God, whose you are, will deliver you out of them. He is your Keeper. He has kept you hitherto. Hold fast to his dear hand, and he will lead you safely through all things.

SAINT FRANCIS DE SALES

ENDURANCE

A Bean-Field Victory

We also pray that you will be strengthened with all his glorious power so you will have all the endurance and patience you need. Colossians 1:11 nlt

Endurance may seem like a strange topic for a book on unemployment. Yet the dictionary defines *endurance* as "the ability to persevere in a task or calling." I never would have considered joblessness a "task" or "calling," but when you're living through the day-in, day-out stresses of this transition time, unemployment is just that. It is a task to handle, an assignment or calling (unwanted though it may be) for a particular time or purpose.

God has been in the calling and assignment business for centuries. He called Noah and gave him the assignment of building an ark. He called Moses and assigned him the task of leading the Israelites. He called Jeremiah, Isaiah, Micah, and others, giving them the assignment to speak His words to people who didn't want to listen. He called Paul with the assignment to take the gospel message to the world. In each instance the calling had nothing to do with the individual's choosing. God took the initiative each time to call each individual to his particular assignment. All of these callings required each individual's ability to persevere until the task was accomplished. All of these callings took endurance.

It's my guess you didn't choose to be unemployed—you didn't choose this awkward transition time in your career. But if that's where you find yourself (and you're God's child), you're probably smack dab in the middle of a calling. Why do I say this? Because God not only calls the Noahs and Jeremiahs and Pauls of this world to fulfill His assignments. He also calls ordinary folks like you, me, and Shammah.

Shammah was an ordinary soldier in David's army. He was assigned a defense position in a bean field that was about ready for harvest. The Philistines, however, had set their sights on Shammah's bean field as the best place to invade the land of Israel. They had armed themselves for a major battle. The Bible says when the Israelite army saw the Philistines coming, they turned tail and ran. All, that is, except Shammah. Shammah had an assignment, a calling to a bean field. So "Shammah took his stand in the middle of the field. He defended it and struck the Philistines down, and the LORD brought about a great victory" (2 Samuel 23:12 NIV).

Shammah was assigned the task of being the best soldier he could possibly be. He fulfilled this calling by refusing to leave the bean field, even when everyone else ran away. And the Lord rewarded Shammah's endurance with a great victory.

Right now unemployment is my calling. I didn't ask for it, but God allowed it. So my current calling requires my endurance, my perseverance, my willingness to stick it out in the bean field of joblessness. As the enemies of discouragement, fear, weariness, worry, and hopelessness invade my territory and send everyone else running, I've decided to remember Shammah. I'll take my stand in my joblessness and strike down those enemies, knowing that the Bible promises the Lord will fight for me. I'll remember my calling and the promise that the Lord will be my strength and the hope that the Lord will deliver me one day and bring about a great victory. I'll fulfill this assignment from God by enduring, just like Shammah.

Will you?

Getting Through Your Day

When life gets really difficult, don't jump to the conclusion that God isn't on the job. Instead, be glad that you are in the very thick of what Christ experienced. This is a spiritual refining process, with glory just around the corner.   1 PETER 4:12–13 MSG

We also boast of our troubles, because we know that trouble produces endurance, endurance brings God's approval, and his approval creates hope.   ROMANS 5:3–4 GNT

You know that the testing of your faith produces steadfastness. And let steadfastness have its full effect, that you may be perfect and complete, lacking in nothing.   JAMES 1:3–4 ESV

Don't throw away your confidence, which has a great reward. For you need endurance, so that after you have done God's will, you may receive what was promised.   HEBREWS 10:35–36 HCSB

Everything that was written in the past was written to teach us, so that through endurance and the encouragement of the Scriptures we might have hope. May the God who gives endurance and encouragement give you a spirit of unity among yourselves as you follow Christ Jesus.   ROMANS 15:4–5 NIV

May the Lord direct your lives as you show God's love and Christ's endurance.   2 THESSALONIANS 3:5 GOD'S WORD

Today I Will Get This Off My Chest...

Use the space below to respond to as many or as few of these questions as you like.

- This joblessness is lasting longer than expected. How does this make you feel? What can the Lord do to help you make it through another day?
- You might question God's motives or actions because your circumstances are difficult. Is this a problem for you? Do you think this attitude comes from unbelief, short-sightedness, or something else?
- Endurance brings with it a sense of accomplishing something. What are you accomplishing during this time of unemployment? What work is God doing in you?
- As days continue without a job, can you ask God for the courage to seek what He has for you in this jobless time even if it is hard, even if it is painful, even if it takes longer than anticipated? Record such a prayer here.

TIMING

At Just the Right Time

Gehazi was telling the king about the time Elisha had brought a boy back to life. At that very moment, the mother of the boy walked in. 2 KINGS 8:5 NLT

I drive a seventeen-year-old Ford station wagon. The roof rack is slightly bent, so the wind whistles through it as the car travels down the street. My mechanic has told me not to drive the car any farther away from home than I care to walk because the car has a tendency to stall and then will refuse to restart for fifteen or twenty minutes. Would I like to replace the car? You betcha. Will I buy another vehicle right now? Not on your life. I'm unemployed, so I still drive that old bomb. It passes inspection. It runs on regular gas. And it's paid for. But will I buy another car someday? I sure hope so! However, it's just not the right time for that now.

When you're unemployed, time and timing are big pieces of your everyday job puzzle. You spend a lot of time looking for work. Then it seems that the one day you apply for a job you find out your application came in too late. The posting was already filled. The time you spent applying now seems to be a waste of time because the timing was all wrong. You've probably also thought that this jobless thing should have been resolved by now. It's been going on too long. And you might have even admitted to friends how long a day seems when no one responds to your e-mails and yet at the same time how fast time seems to be flying by as you watch your financial reserves dwindle.

The timing thing has always been a problem for folks, whether living today or living in Bible times. But, as God's child, you can rest easier when faced with the frustrations of timing if you remember one thing: even when it appears God's plan is taking too much time, God is always *on* time.

Ask Abraham's servant. He traveled for weeks to find the bride God had chosen for Abraham's son Isaac. He happened to arrive at a well *at the exact time* Isaac's bride-to-be was coming to water her sheep.

Ask the disciples. While sailing across the Sea of Galilee a terrible storm threatened to swamp their boat. *At that exact instant* Jesus came walking across the water and calmed the wind and waves.

Ask the Shunnamite woman. Her son had been restored to life by the prophet Elisha. Seven years later she went to see the king to have a property dispute settled. Elisha's servant was standing at the king's throne *at that exact moment* telling him about this very woman and her son.

Are all these coincidences? No. God orchestrated the details that brought these pieces together at the right time so that His plan could unfold in the right way. And it's the same for you. When things aren't working out at the exact time you feel they should be, stop. Consider. It might be that God's timetable is different from yours, but God will bring the pieces of your timing puzzle together in a perfect way.

So when God's time is right, I'll replace that old station wagon. When God's time is right, I'll get that new job. As always, God can be trusted. As always, His timing is perfect. He has never been late for anything, and He's not about to start being late now.

Getting Through Your Day

Do not overlook this one fact, beloved, that with the Lord one day is as a thousand years, and a thousand years as one day.

2 PETER 3:8 ESV

Like an open book, you watched me grow from conception to birth; all the stages of my life were spread out before you, the days of my life all prepared before I'd even lived one day.

PSALM 139:16 MSG

As for me, I trust in You, O LORD, I say, "You are my God." My times are in Your hand.

PSALM 31:14–15 NASB

LORD, how long will I live? When will I die? Tell me how soon my life will end. How short you have made my life! In your sight my lifetime seems nothing. Indeed every living being is no more than a puff of wind, no more than a shadow. All we do is for nothing; we gather wealth, but don't know who will get it. What, then, can I hope for, LORD? I put my hope in you.

PSALM 39:4–7 GNT

Some of you say, "Today or tomorrow we will go to some city. We will stay there a year, do business, and make money." But you do not know what will happen tomorrow! Your life is like a mist. You can see it for a short time, but then it goes away. So you should say, "If the Lord wants, we will live and do this or that."

JAMES 4:13–15 NCV

Teach us to number each of our days so that we may grow in wisdom.

PSALM 90:12 GOD'S WORD

Today I Will...

✓ Be thankful for the reminder that all my times are in God's hands. Nothing can happen to me outside of His timetable for my life.

✓ Be grateful for the example of those in Scripture who witness to me that God will bring together the details of His plan for my life at just the right time.

✓ Appreciate the delays as well as the times that I move ahead in my job search realizing that both the steps and stops of my life are orchestrated by God.

✓ Be pleased to remember that even though this unemployment time often feels like there's a roaring lion behind me and a raging fire in front of me, God has heard my requests. He is at work on my behalf.

✓ Be glad for the assurance of Genesis 18:25 (NIV)—"Will not the Judge of all the earth do right?"

✓ Value this time of unemployment. In this time of job loss I have been able to trust God more as I wait for His timing.

GOD'S PROVISION

Manna from Heaven

My God shall supply all your need according to His riches in glory by Christ Jesus. PHILIPPIANS 4:19 NKJV

Last week a woman approached me at church, handed me an envelope, and said, "I hope this helps." Then she gave me a hug and was gone. I looked inside the envelope to find a grocery store gift card. I was surprised by the woman's generosity, and I shook my head in wonder. God had provided for our needs.

I had been praying for God's provision, yet it was easy for the daily concerns of my joblessness to rob me of seeing His answers to my prayer. I was so full of questions—*Was I looking for work in the right places? Was I supposed to be doing something, going somewhere, talking to someone? Had I missed something? Is that why I was still unemployed after all this time?*—so full of questions I had been missing His answers.

So the unexpected happened. God provided. But He didn't provide in the way I thought He would. I guess that's why I was surprised. He didn't send a job, an interview, or a response to a resume. Instead God provided for my needs in an unusual, unexpected way—with a grocery gift card. That gift card was, for me, like the Israelites' manna from heaven.

When God guided the Israelites through the wilderness there came a time when His people ran out of food. It looked like they would starve. But God had other plans. He is known in the Bible as Jehovah Jireh, which is translated "the Lord will provide." When the Israelites ran out of food, that's exactly what God—Jehovah Jireh—did. He provided for his people in an unusual, unexpected way. God sent manna from heaven, a flaky substance that could be made into bread so God's people wouldn't go hungry.

Now here was a grocery card, my family's manna from heaven. We wouldn't go hungry either. As I looked at the amount it appeared to be more than we needed. But then I laughed. It wasn't too much after all. In three weeks we were expecting some houseguests. The little bit extra in the gift card would cover the extra food we would need to purchase to feed those guests. God had provided, alright, and He had provided based on our need for the month, not just on our need for that day.

As I began to say thanks I recalled other ways God had been providing for us. Ways that I, in my jobless anxiety, had missed seeing at first. Two temporary jobs had helped pay the mortgage payment. A tree limb had fallen, missing the power line by mere inches, but falling within a foot of where the brush would have to be piled for the rubbish pickup. Our ancient station wagon had fired up and rolled into church that day without hesitation. Each overlooked happening was a clear indicator of God's provision in our lives. God *was* answering my prayers. I was just missing it because His provision was coming in unusual, unexpected ways.

I left church that morning with a clearer understanding of God as Jehovah Jireh, my provider. Because He knows my needs, I can trust Him to provide just what I need when I need it. It may come in an unusual, unexpected way, but God will provide. His name guarantees it.

Getting Through Your Day

Those who sow in tears shall reap with shouts of joy! He who goes out weeping, bearing the seed for sowing, shall come home with shouts of joy, bringing his sheaves with him. PSALM 126:5–6 ESV

The LORD God is our sun and our shield. He gives us grace and glory. The LORD will withhold no good thing from those who do what is right. PSALM 84:11 NLT

Our fathers trusted in You; they trusted, and You delivered them. They cried to You, and were delivered; they trusted in You, and were not ashamed. PSALM 22:4–5 NKJV

LORD God, you made the skies and the earth with your very great power. There is nothing too hard for you to do. JEREMIAH 32:17 NCV

By his divine power, God has given us everything we need for living a godly life. We have received all of this by coming to know him, the one who called us to himself by means of his marvelous glory and excellence. 2 PETER 1:3 NLT

God is able to give you more than you need, so that you will always have all you need for yourselves and more than enough for every good cause. 2 CORINTHIANS 9:8 GNT

Jesus replied, "What is impossible with men is possible with God." LUKE 18:27 NIV

Today I Will...

✓ Work on my focus. If I have teenage eyes when it comes to seeing God's provision, I will ask God to help me with my focus. (Teenagers often look past something that is in plain sight. Moms call it "teenage eyes.") His provision is there. I will look for it.

✓ Make a list of God's daily provisions in my life. They may be large or small. But I'll list them all as God brings them to my remembrance. And I will thank Him for each one.

✓ Remind myself not to get so caught up in the concerns of life that my relationship with God suffers. God needs to be my priority. The Bible promises if I seek His kingdom first, everything I need will be given to me as well (see Matthew 6:33).

✓ Take time to do a Bible study on God's provision for His children, looking for parallels in my own life. (Start with Abraham's ram in the thicket; the Israelites' manna, water, and quail; or the widow with the unending supply of oil.)

✓ Pray for wisdom to recognize that God's delay in providing a job for me is not necessarily a denial of my request. It may just be a timing issue.

✓ Copy Philippians 4:19 onto a card or piece of paper. I'll keep that verse as a reminder that Jehovah Jireh is my provider.

BLESSINGS

The Unexpected Experience of Blessings

Is this what you were expecting? Then count yourselves fortunate! LUKE 7:23 MSG

I'll admit it. I wasn't happy about cooking. Before being unemployed, I used to eat most of my meals out in restaurants or fast-food joints. It was almost a necessity, too, because I'm not an iron chef in the kitchen. Let's face it. I'm not a chef of any kind. But being paycheck-less has cut into my discretionary cash flow, so last week I decided to try my hand at refried beans.

I enjoy a good Mexican meal. While I recognized preparing something like enchiladas or guacamole was probably out of my league, I figured anyone could re-fry some beans. I carefully sorted some beans, looking for pebbles (only one in a one-pound bag!), then soaked those little guys overnight. The next morning, as directed by the package, I drained and refilled the pot and set everything boiling on the stovetop. Lips smacking, I couldn't wait for the finished product.

But that's where things started to go downhill. I didn't realize that beans have a mind of their own. If they are cooked improperly, they will refuse to adapt themselves to any recipe. In my case the little monsters wouldn't mash correctly, they wouldn't incorporate the butter, and they wouldn't fry, much less re-fry, correctly in the pan. This wasn't what I had expected. Now my investment in time, energy, beans, and water was a burnt mess.

I shared my bean story later that day with some friends who took pity on me and bought me lunch. As we chatted, my friends smiled at my complaints about being unemployed. Then one of them chuckled and said, "This unemployment thing sure is an unexpected blessing, isn't it?"

Unemployment an unexpected blessing? I'd never looked at this transition time in *those* terms before, so I asked Jason to clarify his comment. Turns out he had had his own experiences with unemployment. He had been frustrated at things not being what he had expected either. But then he remembered the Bible says when things aren't what you expect, you should count yourself fortunate. Hidden within those unexpected happenings might just be some hidden blessings waiting to be discovered. In Jason's case his unemployment time had given him more free time to be with his children—to take them to school, to linger with them over breakfast, to attend daytime programs or ball games.

As he talked I realized other friends had mentioned something similar during their times of unemployment. Derek had found the blessing of being involved in a youth ministry. Mike had been blessed to sit with a homebound neighbor at a moment's notice. Frank had been able to finish up some chores that had been piling up at home. Shirley had been blessed with some much-needed rest. All these unexpected blessings were hidden within the unexpected experience of unemployment.

The Bible says, "God richly gives us everything to enjoy" (1 Timothy 6:17 NCV). And guess what? Everything means *everything*, including this job transition time. God has allowed this time of unemployment in your life. If your joblessness isn't what you expected it to be, hear God's Word say to you, "Count yourself fortunate!" Then take this reminder to heart: there's probably an unexpected blessing hidden within this unexpected time of unemployment. Ask God to open your eyes to see it.

Getting Through Your Day

How blessed is everyone who fears the LORD, who walks in His ways. When you shall eat of the fruit of your hands, you will be happy and it will be well with you. PSALM 128:1–2 NASB

"Bring the full 10 percent into the storehouse so that there may be food in My house. Test Me in this way," says the LORD of Hosts. "See if I will not open the floodgates of heaven and pour out a blessing for you without measure." MALACHI 3:10 HCSB

The LORD bless you and protect you; the LORD make His face shine on you, and be gracious to you; the LORD look with favor on you and give you peace. NUMBERS 6:24–26 HCSB

Here is what I have found out: the best thing we can do is eat and drink and enjoy what we have worked for during the short life that God has given us; this is our fate. If God gives us wealth and property and lets us enjoy them, we should be grateful and enjoy what we have worked for. It is a gift from God. ECCLESIASTES 5:18–19 GNT

The LORD will make you the head, not the tail. If you pay attention to the commands of the LORD your God that I give you this day and carefully follow them, you will always be at the top, never at the bottom. DEUTERONOMY 28:13 NIV

Blessed are those who hunger and thirst for righteousness, for they shall be satisfied. Blessed are the merciful, for they shall receive mercy. Blessed are the pure in heart, for they shall see God. MATTHEW 5:6–8 ESV

Today I Will Pray...

✓ For the willingness to look at my situation from God's eyes—to see as He sees—and so trust Him more.

✓ For an opportunity to use some of my extra time during my joblessness as a means of ministry to others, knowing that in so doing I'll feel useful and fulfilled.

✓ For eyes to see the blessings around me and to humbly thank God for the unexpected blessings in the midst of my unexpected circumstances.

✓ For a renewed outlook and a positive attitude that can replace negative words or thoughts with positive ones, recognizing there is godly power in optimism, a medicinal quality in cheerfulness (see Proverbs 17:22).

✓ For the wisdom to remember that no life is ever perfect. Everyone has troubles sometime. The way to get through this time is with a deeper trust in God and a closer personal relationship with Him.

✓ For the ability to recognize the small things in life as God's blessings in disguise—the kind words of a friend, the store clerk's smile, the collision I avoided at the stop sign. (God's blessings may be big ones—like that new job one day—but many of His blessings are small and surround you already. Just look.)

PERSONALIZE THE RIDE

Use this space to clarify and record your thoughts. By this point in your ride you probably understand this will be a good reminder of your thoughts later on, and you know that you can answer as few or as many of these questions as you like.

- How does it make you feel to wait for God's timing in your career transition?
- How does what you have learned about endurance affect you?
- Is there something you want to tell God about His provision for you?
- Is there a way you can share your blessings with others?
- I am thankful today for... (There is always something to thank God for!)

6

COMING INTO THE STATION

After twisting and twirling through the ups and downs and black tunnels of my first ride on the Dragon Coaster, I almost came to tears when I glimpsed the roller coaster's station. Coming off that last bunny hill and around a switchback turn, there was the ride's terminus, mere feet away. My horror was almost at an end. If you'll recall, I was only seven years old, and the Dragon Coaster had been my first roller-coaster ride. But I can still remember that feeling of finally coming into the station. I knew from watching the television advertisement that soon the coaster car's brakes would lock, the movement would end, and all the riders would disembark at the station. That glimpse of the station was just what I needed to survive the last segment of the ride.

If you've ever been in an amusement park and watched the goings on at a roller-coaster ride, you've probably noticed there are many folks who share my seven-year-old sense of relief as they clank and roll back into the coaster station. Faces that mere moments before had been wrenched in grimaces will now relax into smiles. Hands that were clenched on safety rails will now be raised in a wave of hello. Voices that had screamed in terror will now be tinged with laughter, or, as in my case, soft sobs of relief. As the roller-coaster car comes into the station, all those riding, watching, or waiting know there is an end in sight to this ride.

The roller coaster of unemployment will have an end too. There will be a time when the coaster car carrying the jobless will come into the station. Sometimes that end will come quickly—my nephew was downsized by his employer but found a replacement job within a month. For some folks the ride will last a bit longer—I've been unemployed for over a year now. But some will find the roller-coaster ride of unemployment will end in an unusual way. Just as some thrill rides deposit riders a few feet before the next embarkation point, those in a career transition time might find their unemployment ride ending in an unusual place or way. For example, one friend never did find work in his field even after a two-year search; he began his own successful business instead.

Indeed, there's a sense of relief when the unemployment ride gives you a glimpse of the station just around the next switchback curve. And just like coaster riders cheer as they reenter the station, you too may want to consider your own cheers, praise, and worship for God as you trust Him to bring you to the end of this unemployment ride. For you see, that's the only way to survive this roller coaster of unemployment. You've got to trust God for the whole ride, beginning to end.

At this point in your unemployment ride, you may have gotten a glimpse of the ride's end at the station, or you may have a bit more track to travel. Either way, God still has some things to say to you in His Word about your self-image, joy, peace, praise, and the strength you'll need to finish this roller-coaster ride of unemployment.

SELF-IMAGE

Tell Yourself the Truth

*He chose us in Him, before the foundation of the world, to be
holy and blameless in His sight.* EPHESIANS 1:4 HCSB

Miss Viola moaned she wasn't worth anything any more because she no longer earned a paycheck. I've often heard that comment from others who have lost their jobs. That's not surprising, though, since the world tends to define individuals by their job, often initiating first contact with the query, "What do you do?" However, the Bible says because work is God's gift to you, your job or career is not the measure of who you are as an individual. Regardless of what society seems to say, you are more than the job.

Did you hear that? I'll say it again: you are more than the job. Right now you may not have work. You may not have a paycheck coming in. Because of that, your emotions may be all over the map. But listen. You are more than the job. In God's eyes you are a valuable individual. You are unique. God says so in His Word.

In Genesis He tells you you're made in His image. John declares you are beloved by Him. Ephesians says you are a child of God, chosen by Him before the world was created, redeemed by Christ's blood, and a full citizen of God's kingdom. First John says you are forgiven by God for all of your sins—past, present, and future. Romans says you have been called for a purpose and have been gifted by God's Spirit to minister to others. The Corinthian letters say you have been set apart by God's Spirit and are God's ambassador to the world. Indeed, you are more than just a job. If you have been defining

133

yourself by the world's standard of what you can do or how much you can earn, you need to start telling yourself the truth.

But it isn't easy. I've listened to the lies of the world inside my head for so long that God's truth about my self-worth seems awkward, forced, or even irrelevant to my situation. When I haven't a clue about how to pay this month's electric bill because there's no money coming in, I find it difficult to trust God because my job was always my source of income and provision. My job made me feel like I was doing something important. Others gave me respect because of my position. Yet is it possible that I had let my work become more than work, more than just a paycheck? Now that I've lost my job I've also lost those other things that made me feel valued and secure. In that realization I see another lie that has crept into my life— the lie that I could rely on a job to give me self-worth or a sense of security when in reality only God can provide these things.

Indeed, the lies are there for everyone. They might be hidden. They might be obvious. But the lies will come to the surface when your reliance and trust in God is tested during this time of joblessness. So use this time to good advantage. Shine God's light on the lies in your life by telling yourself the truth. You are more than your job. You are accepted, secure, and beloved by God. You are never far from His presence. And *you* are valuable to God. Now that's the truth.

Getting Through Your Day

You were taught to leave your old self—to stop living the evil way you lived before. That old self becomes worse, because people are fooled by the evil things they want to do. But you were taught to be made new in your hearts, to become a new person. That new person is made to be like God—made to be truly good and holy.
Ephesians 4:22–24 NCV

You made all the delicate, inner parts of my body and knit me together in my mother's womb. Thank you for making me so wonderfully complex! Your workmanship is marvelous—how well I know it. PSALM 139:13–14 NLT

Do you not know that your body is a temple of the Holy Spirit, who is in you, whom you have received from God? You are not your own; you were bought at a price. Therefore honor God with your body. 1 CORINTHIANS 6:19–20 NIV

We are His creation—created in Christ Jesus for good works, which God prepared ahead of time so that we should walk in them. EPHESIANS 2:10 HCSB

He chose us in Him before the foundation of the world, that we would be holy and blameless before Him. EPHESIANS 1:4 NASB

Before I shaped you in the womb, I knew all about you. Before you saw the light of day, I had holy plans for you. JEREMIAH 1:5 MSG

Today I Will Get This Off My Chest...

Use the space below to respond to as few or as many of these questions as you like.

- How have your feelings of self-esteem survived during this career transition time? Do you define yourself in terms of *what you do* rather than in terms of *who you are*? Why?
- While you may be a spouse, parent, friend, relative, or volunteer, how does it make you feel to realize you are more than that to God? That you are important to

Him, created to be unique and necessary to His plan for the world?

- What has to change in your life so that you can begin to tell yourself the truth about yourself?
- Have you been relying on your job or earthly possession to fulfill and satisfy you? Is this dependence and reliance holding you captive? What is God showing you that has undermined His rightful priority in your life?

JOY

A Candy Cascade

Rejoice in the Lord always; again I will say, rejoice!
PHILIPPIANS 4:4 NASB

It was well past noon. The cup of coffee and day-old cinnamon roll that I had gulped down at sunrise had long since worn off. My stomach was rumbling, yet the church service was still in progress. I quietly reached for a small candy to still my growling stomach.

Unfortunately, my fingers fumbled the job. The package of candies split wide open, spilling the unwrapped sweets onto the gently sloping floor beneath the pew in front of me. With a plinkety-plunkety abandon, the candies gathered speed as they bounced and rolled away from me, heading toward the front of the auditorium. I noticed people in front of me glancing toward the floor as the candies made a speedy advance past their shoes. Some folks even turned around to see who might have started such a candy cascade.

I felt my pew begin to jiggle and caught sight of my family. Seated next to me, they had observed my plight but had been unable to corral the errant sweets. Their response to the situation was not embarrassment, however, but merriment. Unfortunately, because we were in church, they had to stifle their mirth. With contorted faces they laughed silently, literally bouncing in the pew, holding their sides, quietly gasping for breath. The whole situation was hilarious.

After the church service, we spent several minutes trying to clean up as much as possible, giggling when we realized that some of the candies had made it to within a few feet of the pastor's podium. Over a shared meal we regaled friends with the full details of the fiasco and laughed aloud until our sides ached.

As we laughed, I realized that for several hours I hadn't worried about being unemployed. I wondered: *Could joy and laughter have made that much of a difference to my day? Could it be that the joy that spilled all over everyone as those candies spilled all over the auditorium banished the burdens that came with joblessness? That such joy could drive depression and anxiety away? That joy could relieve the stress of limited finances and few resources?* It sure seemed that way.

The apostle Paul would agree. When he was chained between two guards in a prison cell his future was unknown, much as yours is when you're riding the roller coaster of unemployment. Yet Paul did not respond to his unknowns with anxiety, depression, or stress. He rejoiced and told others to do the same. Paul knew deep down that "the joy of the LORD is your strength" (Nehemiah 8:10 NIV).

As I thought about that candy cascade and the joy-filled day that followed it, I determined in my heart to start my next unemployed week with a new purpose. When I don't get my way, when I don't get a response to an e-mail, when I don't see a job on the horizon, I'll respond with a song to God. When I find my skills discounted, my experience devalued, and my situation diminished by others, I'll raise a chorus of praise to the Lord. And when I'm buried under a load of dreary responsibilities, depressing unknowns, and devastating financial reversals, I'll choose to rejoice in God my Savior, for there is God-promised strength in God-centered joy. I've got the candy to prove it!

Getting Through Your Day

The Lord is my strength and my shield; my heart trusts in him, and I am helped. My heart leaps for joy and I will give thanks to him in song.   Psalm 28:7 NIV

You that are righteous, be glad and rejoice because of what the Lord has done. You that obey him, shout for joy!
                                                       Psalm 32:11 GNT

Make a joyful noise to the Lord, all the earth! Serve the Lord with gladness! Come into his presence with singing!
                                                     Psalm 100:1–2 ESV

A twinkle in the eye means joy in the heart, and good news makes you feel fit as a fiddle.   Proverbs 15:30 MSG

Even if the fig tree does not bloom and the vines have no grapes, even if the olive tree fails to produce and the fields yield no food, even if the sheep pen is empty and the stalls have no cattle—even then, I will be happy with the Lord. I will truly find joy in God, who saves me.
                                          Habakkuk 3:17–18 God's Word

You have shown me the way of life, and you will fill me with the joy of your presence.   Acts 2:28 NLT

Today I Will...

✓ Spend some time in joyful thanksgiving, recalling the events of the past week that made me smile. The joy of remembering the Lord's hand on my life will give me strength to face another week.

✓ Take some time to get some exercise. Endorphins are released and the body is de-stressed with vigorous exercise like lifting weights, taking long walks, shooting hoops, gardening, and cleaning house. The joy found in this de-stressing will relieve my feelings of depression and anxiety.

✓ Talk to a friend or family member and compare notes about what brings us joy and laughter. The joy found in sharing such stories will give my attitude about my life a boost.

✓ Write down a Bible verse that makes me smile. I will place it where I will see it often, knowing that the joy found in remembering God's Word will refresh my spirit.

✓ Share a comfort food with a friend or family member. The joy found in tasting this food will remind me that the sweetest joys are often found in simple things.

✓ Sing a joyful song—even if I forget the words, even if I can't carry a tune in a bucket. The joy found in singing will bring me hope and optimism for what lies ahead.

PEACE

Waiting for Peace

May the Lord of peace himself give you peace at all times and in every way. 2 THESSALONIANS 3:16 NIV

I find I'm not very peaceable these days. Rather, I'm impatient, easily disturbed, and openly unsettled. In my mind I've been unemployed way too long. I want my new job, and I want it now. (There's not much peace in that statement, is there?) I ask God to work on my behalf and guide me in my job search. But when He takes too long, when I can't see clearly what He has in mind, I take matters into my own hands. I push on a closed door and force it open. I follow a lead that isn't even there or apply for jobs I'm not qualified for only to meet with rejection. I take my frustration out on others when I can't get past the e-mail hiring gateway of a company's personnel department. I end up irritated and weary when really what I need is a good dose of peace. Sound familiar?

Despite living during an unpeaceful time in Jewish history, the prophet Ezekiel managed to survive peacefully with the Jewish captives in Babylon. Sometimes he had odd dreams and visions, like the one of a wheel within a wheel. Sometimes he did strange things, like eating a parchment scroll that contained the words of God. But then sometimes he did nothing, like the time he sat by the river for seven days without saying or doing anything. Strange. Odd. Unusual. But the Bible says after that week-long sitting spell, "the word of the LORD came to [Ezekiel]" (Ezekiel 3:16 NIV). Ezekiel waited in peace for God to come to him, and God did—in God's time and in God's way.

It seems that doing things Ezekiel's way might be strange by some folks' standards, but in God's economy, Ezekiel's way of life was a lot more peaceful. Why? Ezekiel recognized that the timing of everything was in the Lord's hands. That's why he could wait for seven days doing nothing and not stress out about it. Because Ezekiel believed God was working out a plan for His people, he could peacefully rest and trust that all was well even though situations changed at a snail's pace. Ezekiel also allowed God's presence and peace to so permeate his life that he never responded to his circumstances with an impatient action.

Is a peaceable life possible when you're unemployed? Yes, it is. While folks might consider you strange, odd, or unusual for meeting the challenges of joblessness with a sense of peace, that's exactly what can happen if you follow Ezekiel's example. Whenever you're tempted to take things into your own hands and do things your own way, remember Ezekiel's week-long sitting spell. Just waiting on God and relinquishing your timetable—even for seven long days—can lead to peace. The Bible also says trusting God for each circumstance leads to peace. Looking back to see God's provision along the way leads to peace. And spending time in God's presence means soaking up peace from the One who is peace personified.

Since God's children should actively pursue the things that lead to peace, why not choose to follow Ezekiel's example during this roller coaster of unemployment. Give God time to be himself with you—to be peace in your midst. Choose to wait for Him. Choose to wait—for peace.

Getting Through Your Day

[Jesus said,] "I've told you all this so that trusting me, you will be unshakable and assured, deeply at peace. In this godless world

you will continue to experience difficulties. But take heart! I've conquered the world." JOHN 16:33 MSG

You, LORD, give perfect peace to those who keep their purpose firm and put their trust in you. ISAIAH 26:3 GNT

[Jesus said,] "Peace I leave with you; My peace I give to you; not as the world gives do I give to you. Do not let your heart be troubled, nor let it be fearful." JOHN 14:27 NASB

Be anxious for nothing, but in everything by prayer and supplication, with thanksgiving, let your requests be made known to God; and the peace of God, which surpasses all understanding, will guard your hearts and minds through Christ Jesus.
PHILIPPIANS 4:6–7 NKJV

Rejoice. Aim for restoration, comfort one another, agree with one another, live in peace; and the God of love and peace will be with you. 2 CORINTHIANS 13:11 ESV

LORD, you establish peace for us; all that we have accomplished you have done for us. ISAIAH 26:12 NIV

Today I Will Remember...

What can make those uneasy whose souls dwell at ease in God? MATTHEW HENRY

The better you become acquainted with God, the [fewer] tensions you feel and the more peace you possess.
CHARLES L. ALLEN

Peace is the full confidence that God is Who He says He is and that He will keep every promise in His Word.

DOROTHY HARRISON PENTECOST

Peace, perfect peace—in this dark world of sin?
The blood of Jesus whispers peace within.

EDWARD H. BICKERSTETH

The night and the storm look as though they will last forever; but calm and the morning cannot be stayed; the storm in its very nature is transient. The effort of nature, as that of the human heart, is to return to its repose, for God is peace.

GEORGE MACDONALD

Drop Thy still dews of quietness till all our striving cease;
Take from our soul the strain and stress,
And let our ordered lives confess
The beauty of Thy Peace.

JOHN GREENLEAF WHITTIER

STRENGTH

Shoulder to Shoulder

*I will give to the peoples purified lips, that all of
them may call on the name of the LORD, to serve Him
shoulder to shoulder.* ZEPHANIAH 3:9 NASB

I recently watched a cheerleading competition that included
building human pyramids. I watched in fascination as the
strongest members of the cheerleading squads quickly dropped
to a hands-and-knees position, shoulder to shoulder with one
another, forming a strong base for the pyramid. As each successive level rose higher, the strongest pyramids were those
that kept this tight formation. I wondered if these athletes had
learned this shoulder to shoulder strength technique from
Nehemiah.

When the Jews returned to their homeland after a seventy-
year prison sentence in Babylon, they found their capital city
in ruins. Jerusalem's walls and gates were non-existent. Most
of the homes inside the city were uninhabitable. God's temple
had been burned and destroyed. Faced with so many pressing
needs, the leader of the refugees, Nehemiah, determined that
their first priority should be to rebuild the city walls.

However, there were outsiders from neighboring cities
who didn't want Jerusalem rebuilt. They had profited from
Jerusalem's destruction, so any change to the status quo could
negatively affect their income. These outsiders used any means
possible to discourage the rebuilders, even threatening their
lives if they continued to fix the walls.

Nehemiah saw fear on his workers' faces and responded
with an old-fashioned pep talk. He reminded the refugees that

they were God's children, that God was with them, and that His joy—found deep down inside their hearts—would provide the strength they needed to rebuild the city.

Then Nehemiah added one other strength-building tactic. He reminded his workers that they were a team, that they weren't in this tough position all alone. Nehemiah suggested that the wall rebuilders work near one another, close enough to rub shoulders. If any worker ran into trouble, he was to blow a trumpet blast. Nehemiah rallied his workers with the battle cry, "Wherever you hear the sound of the trumpet, join us there. Our God will fight for us!" (Nehemiah 4:20 NIV). With this shoulder-to-shoulder strength strategy in place, Nehemiah and his crew were able to successfully rebuild Jerusalem's walls in fifty-two days.

Unfortunately, I've fallen so deeply into the societal habit of self-sufficiency, I often forget Nehemiah's strength tactic of working shoulder to shoulder. I often hesitate to call on anyone for anything—even in an emergency. Because of my own self-reliance I never sound the trumpet, so I end up fighting my battles with fear, discouragement, and spiritual decline all on my own. My over-resourcefulness becomes a tool that works against me, cutting me off from God's strength and the strength of others.

Just as the human-pyramid cheerleaders and the Jerusalem refugees found strength from building shoulder to shoulder, you can find God-given strength from standing shoulder to shoulder with God's children. How? By praying for one another and sharing conversations and encouragement together, you'll be cheered, invigorated, and comforted. By watching others overcome difficulties, you'll be able to bear your own trials better and trust God more confidently. And as you approach the end of this roller-coaster ride, you'll be able to look back and see that your spiritual strength has grown. You can walk with God with more faith and trust, all because you learned to stand shoulder to shoulder with other believers during a tough time in your life.

So... wanna build a pyramid?

Getting Through Your Day

It is God who arms me with strength and makes my way perfect. He makes my feet like the feet of a deer; he enables me to stand on the heights. 2 SAMUEL 22:33–34 NIV

Blessed are those whose strength is in you, who have set their hearts on pilgrimage... They go from strength to strength, till each appears before God in Zion. PSALM 84:5, 7 NIV

I can do all things through him who strengthens me. PHILIPPIANS 4:13 ESV

Be alert. Be firm in the Christian faith. Be courageous and strong. 1 CORINTHIANS 16:13 GOD'S WORD

Build up your strength in union with the Lord and by means of his mighty power. EPHESIANS 6:10 GNT

I pray that from his glorious, unlimited resources he will empower you with inner strength through his Spirit. Then Christ will make his home in your hearts as you trust in him. Your roots will grow down into God's love and keep you strong. EPHESIANS 3:16–17 NLT

But my people—oh, I'll make them strong, God-strong! and they'll live my way. ZECHARIAH 10:12 MSG

Today I Will Pray For...

✓ A way to apply the strength found in teamwork to my solitary situation of joblessness. Nehemiah's wall builders gained more strength by working closely alongside others. Understanding this principle will help me on this unemployment ride.

✓ An acceptance of my weaknesses. I cannot do everything, and I cannot do a lot of things on my own. I need others and the help they can give. I need God's help and the strength He provides.

✓ An increased faith. I must believe that God wants to strengthen me during this time, that He willingly stands ready to empower me when I am weak.

✓ Eyes to observe and learn from the examples of others. As I see others overcome difficulties, I will be better able to bear my own trials better and trust God more confidently.

✓ God to provide a network of His children to stand with me during my unemployment. Such a support group will help me walk more closely with God as we pray, share, and grow stronger together.

✓ God's strength to flow from me to others. As I am able to give to someone else during this transition time, I'll find cheerfulness, comfort, and refreshment.

PRAISE AND WORSHIP

Before the End

*Ascribe to the LORD the glory of His name; bring an offering
and come before Him. Worship the LORD in the splendor
of [His] holiness.* 1 CHRONICLES 16:29 HCSB

Is there anything better to do when you come to the end of a
rough patch than to take some time to praise the Lord? No,
indeed. Just consider the ancient Israelites.

After traversing the wilderness for forty years, they crossed
the Jordan River and were instructed to set up some large
stones on Mt. Ebal to use as an altar of sacrifice. This was to be
their place to praise and worship the Lord. According to Deuteronomy this altar was to be simple in structure—just stacked
stones coated with plaster. No architects or skilled workers
were needed to construct this worship place. It was so simply
built a child could do it. And that was the message God wanted
to convey. Praise and worship should be a simple thing.

But if you skim over this story too quickly, there's one not-
so-small piece of the puzzle you might miss in this picture.
You must realize this altar on Mt. Ebal was set up *before* the
Promised Land had been fully conquered, *before* the land was
under the control of the Israelites. This place of praise and
worship came into being *before* the end to their hard work,
their rough patch, their trying time. And that was a message
God wanted to convey. Praise and worship should not only be
a simple thing; it should also be an all-the-time, no-matter-
what's-happening, before-you-see-the-end-of-it thing. Praise
and worship for God should resound in your heart even before

149

you get to the end of your rough patch, even before your roller-coaster ride of unemployment ends.

Why? Because there's always something to praise the Lord for. When the Israelites left Egypt and were still years away from the land God had promised them, Moses sang a song of praise in the desert to worship God for His miracle of throwing horses and riders into the sea. Hannah worshiped the Lord when all she had was a promise of a child, when Samuel hadn't even been conceived. Jonah praised the Lord from inside the whale without a glimpse of deliverance in sight. Shadrach, Meshach, and Abednego praised God even with a super-heated furnace blasting them in the face, even before the Lord himself joined them in that fiery place.

Each one of these people recognized both the simplicity and before-the-fact needfulness of praising God. When you praise the Lord—even when there's no end to the rough patch, even when the job offers haven't come rolling in—you are proclaiming your trust in who God says He is, your faith in what He has promised to do, and your gratefulness for the things He has already accomplished for you. While it might be hard to praise and worship while you're still in the midst of the roller-coaster ride of unemployment, the Bible says this sacrifice of praise honors God and opens the way for Him to bring about His direction in your life.

As you and I wait for the roller coaster of unemployment to come into that final station, let's remember that God is worthy of our trust. He is worthy of our praise. Let's lift our hearts and hands in worship. Let's just praise the Lord—*before* the end of the ride.

Getting Through Your Day

Through Jesus we should always bring God a sacrifice of praise, that is, words that acknowledge him.

HEBREWS 13:15 GOD'S WORD

I will exalt you, my God the King; I will praise your name for ever and ever. Every day I will praise you and extol your name for ever and ever. Great is the LORD and most worthy of praise; his greatness no one can fathom.

PSALM 145:1–3 NIV

Oh come, let us worship and bow down; let us kneel before the LORD, our Maker! For he is our God, and we are the people of his pasture, and the sheep of his hand.

PSALM 95:6–7 ESV

My soul will make its boast in the LORD; the humble will hear it and rejoice. O magnify the LORD with me, and let us exalt His name together. I sought the LORD, and He answered me, and delivered me from all my fears.

PSALM 34:2–4 NASB

Sing to the LORD! Praise his name! Day after day announce that the LORD saves his people. Tell people about his glory. Tell all the nations about his miracles. The LORD is great! He should be highly praised.

PSALM 96:2–4 GOD'S WORD

Then I heard all creatures in heaven and on earth and under the earth and in the sea saying: "To the One who sits on the throne and to the Lamb be praise and honor and glory and power forever and ever."

REVELATION 5:13 NCV

Today I Will...

✓ Be thankful that praise and worship doesn't require a special formula, place, or time of day. My praise can bubble up from my heart as easily and simply as a child's giggle.

✓ Be grateful for the reminder that my praise and worship of the Lord should resound in my heart all the time, no matter what's happening.

✓ Appreciate that God is glorified when I worship Him and honored when I thank Him. He is exalted when I place my trust in Him and what He has promised to do. And He is blessed by my praise.

✓ Be pleased to remember that Moses, Hannah, Jonah, Shadrach, Meshach, and Abednego praised and worshiped God before the final outcome of their situations, knowing that I should do the same.

✓ Be glad that while the praise and worship of God is to be a simple thing, it also embodies many elements like trust, joy, confession, reverence, gratefulness, and the remembrance of His Word.

✓ Value the reminder that God is worthy of my worship, praise, and trust even when there is no end to my unemployment ride in sight.

PERSONALIZE THE RIDE

Use this space to clarify and record your thoughts about this last chapter in your ride. These last recollections will be a good reminder of how things affected you during this ride. Consider these questions to get started:

- Are you filled with peace today? Why or why not?
- Are you joyful about what is on your plate right now? Why or why not?
- What do you want God to know today about your sense of self-worth? Be honest.
- Is there an action you can take to garner more of God's strength?
- I am thankful today for… (There is always something to praise and worship God for!)

Epilogue

THIRTY-ONE-derful REMINDERS

Your ride on this roller coaster of unemployment has brought you through thirty-one reminders to trust God in this transition time. But these wonderful reminders are powerless pages of black ink on white paper unless you're assured that you are God's child. What do I mean?

The Bible tells us that God loves everyone. More specifically, God loves you. In fact God loves you so much He wants you to be His child, to rely on Him because He has good plans for you.

But the Bible also says you can't have this life plan if sin stands between you and God. Sin—all the bad things people do—builds a wall between you and God. Unfortunately God's penalty for sin is death. Yet God doesn't want you to die, so He has provided an alternative. The Bible says if you acknowledge your sin, turn away from it, and accept *Jesus'* death on the cross as God's only acceptable payment for *your* sin, God will grant you forgiveness, eternal life in heaven, and the assurance that you are His child.

If you want this assurance, if you want this book's thirty-one-derful reminders of trust to make a difference in your life, you'll need to pray with your whole heart:

Dear God, I know I am a sinner. I need your forgiveness. I want to turn away from my sins. I believe that Jesus, your

Son, died on the cross to save me from my sins and that you raised Him to live eternally. In your power I put my trust in Him and make Him my Lord and Savior. Amen.

With that short, heartfelt prayer, you get heaven; you get forgiveness; you get all thirty-one-derful ways God stands ready to help you through this transition time. The choice is yours. I hope you'll choose Him.

—S. M. Hupp

ADDITIONAL RESOURCES

The following resources may be helpful in your job search.

BOOKS

Career Crossover: Leaving the Marketplace for Ministry by Tom R. Harper, B & H Publishing Group, 2007.

Cure for the Common Life: Living in Your Sweet Spot by Max Lucado, W. Publishing Group, a Division of Thomas Nelson, Inc., 2005.

Forty-Eight Days to the Work You Love by Dan Miller, Broadman & Holman Publishers, 2005.

No More Mondays by Dan Miller, Waterbrook Press, 2008.

What Color Is Your Parachute 2010: Job Hunting in Hard Times by Richard Nelson Bolles, Ten Speed Press, Berkeley, CA, 2009.

WEB SITES

(Note: some sites have subscription costs. This list is intended only as a reference tool and is in no way an endorsement of the site. Always be careful about sharing personal or financial information online.)

Specific Companies

Look up specific company Web sites; search for a careers or job path for openings.

General Job Sites

Career Builders: www.careerbuilder.com
Craigslist: www.craigslist.org
Executive Positions: www.theladders.com
Freelance / Consulting Jobs: www.sologig.com
Indeed: www.indeed.com
Jobs: www.jobster.com
Military: www.recruitmilitary.com/jobsearch/search.asp
Monster: www.monster.com
Retail: www.allretailjobs.com
Simply Hired: www.simplyhired.com
Technology: www.dice.com

Christian

To find jobs in Christian ministry or churches, try these Web sites:
www.churchstaff.com
www.churchjobs.com
www.pastorfinder.com
www.pastorsearch.com
www.christianjobs.com

Government Jobs

http://jobsearch.usajobs.opm.gov
FBI: http://fbijobs.gov
Post Office: www.usps.com/employment

ALTERNATIVE JOB OPPORTUNITIES

With more people facing unemployment, you might try:

- Temp agencies (such as www.manpower.jobs.com; www.kellyservices.com, www.nettemps.com, www.us. randstad.com)

- Get paid to be a subject in a medical or clinical trial or for participating in research studies at a large medical center near you. Sell your blood plasma to a blood bank.
- Substitute teach (apply online at your local public school system or in person at the personnel department)
- Do odd jobs. Be a dog-walker, grass-cutter, or leaf-raker. Be an in-home caregiver for a few hours each week.
- Sell personal items on Craig's List, eBay, at a consignment store, or yard sale. Rent out a room in your home. Turn your hobby into cash by making stuff to sell.

NOTE TO THE READER

The publisher invites you to share your response to the message of this book by writing Discovery House Publishers, P.O. Box 3566, Grand Rapids, MI 49501, U.S.A. For information about other Discovery House books, music, videos, or DVDs, contact us at the same address or call 1-800-653-8333. Find us on the Internet at http://www.dhp.org/ or send e-mail to books@dhp.org.